T0105649

ESSAYS IN HOLISTIC
SOCIAL WORK PRACTICE

ESSAYS IN HOLISTIC
SOCIAL WORK PRACTICE

THE NEED FOR AN INTERDISCIPLINARY APPROACH

—————— *by* ——————

Allan Mohl, Ph.D.

authorHOUSE®

AuthorHouse™
1663 Liberty Drive
Bloomington, IN 47403
www.authorhouse.com
Phone: 1 (800) 839-8640

Published by AuthorHouse 11/04/2015

ISBN: 978-1-5049-4819-7 (sc)
ISBN: 978-1-5049-4820-3 (hc)
ISBN: 978-1-5049-4818-0 (e)

Library of Congress Control Number: 2015914526

CONTENTS

CHAPTER I

Introduction:
An Epidemiological Focus

The following Project covers many years of experience. What this author has attempted to do is to present theoretical and pragmatic treatment models which have evolved from 18 years of experience in various social service settings.

They reflect an epidemiological focus which is a systems approach to treatment and the boundaries to be worked on can vary from a family to an entire community.

This Independent Study Project is based on the assumption that the profession's survival is dependent on its adaptability and accountability and this carries implications for practice. The fragmented use of methodologies, meanings and manpower are too often subject to whim, personal and professional bias, and often to what is thought of as professional self-interest. Ironically, this self-interest has not proved to be well-served considering public attitudes toward social work services, limited social work job opportunities, uneven successes in licensing, declassification of social work positions and rapidly decreasing funds for social work education. Even considering the terrible social attitudes and political behavior in the country in these difficult times, social work's troubles may also be attributable to its lack in accountability. It may be necessary for social workers to challenge the historic ways of viewing practice to better assure their future.

As Bartlett and others have pointed out, the history of social work practice is really a history of method or technical development.[1] Richmond herself recommended, for example, that caseworkers go to work in private family agencies so that they could select their clients for the purpose of developing and refining the casework method.[2] With all due deference, that advice did little to alert caseworkers to professional accountability. Methods and skills became equated with practice and even with social work. The honing of methods became an end as well as a means. Proliferating methods and skills became central in the professional education curriculum, and methods even became the primary focus of researchers, who continually seek to find out whether and how they work.[3] Inventions of new methods continue, and students cry for more skills.

In essence, social workers must be able to recognize that linkage with other disciplines and with different agencies and services are essential in treating the total individual. This invariably entails a macrosystemic approach in order to help individuals in that the practitioner is working with a multiplicity of systems which are linked to each other and which effect the individual client.

The many-tiered crises of the 1960s generated many changes in social work in the 1970s and 80s. Perhaps foremost among these were conceptual changes. Beginning in 1970, practice materials began to appear as social work, instead of casework, group work, family treatment, and community organization approaches. This was more than a semantic difference. The intention was to assume a professional stance, based on knowledge as well as skills, in regard to what social work was doing, to focus at last on the phenomena, the substance of the professional commitment, and to allow these phenomena to determine the most suitable methodology to be used.

As Bartlett said so clearly in The <u>Common Base of Social Work Practice</u>, the situation will generate the tasks to be accomplished, and no longer did social work have to be imprisoned in its methodological perspectives.[4] For all those years social work had been offering its well-honed methods to those who could use them instead of first finding out what was needed and then selecting the method from its repertoire or inventing new methods.

The next step in the evolution of social work practice leads quite naturally then in the direction of accountability.[5] From an emphasis on methods, the profession has moved to an orientation in which methods become the servants rather than the masters of practice activities. After all, the "what" of practice is as much a part of practice formulations as the "how." Perhaps it is now time to apply social work knowledge, values and skills to an epidemiological orientation. This orientation has the potential of unifying the fragmented approaches and commitments; but, perhaps most important, it can be demonstrated to be a rational step toward accountability.

However, there are constraints that flow from the use of this perspective, and social workers have to be clear about the implications in order to make an informed choice about how they want to practice their profession. First, an epidemiological orientation using an ecosystems perspective on practice places a formidable burden on social work knowledge. Depending on the areas of expertise or specialization of social workers and location in the system of services, they will need to know about social systems, legal, educational, religious and medical institutions, relevant policy, political trends, the structure of services and network systems of services and how they affect populations, and the populations before them - not only populations at risk, but so-called integrated, well functioning individuals as well. They will have to know how to apply systems principles and the ecological metaphor.[6] Intellectual assessment skills will have to coexist with empathic and interviewing skills.

A second requirement of this perspective is that social workers will have to take more seriously the matter of research. This refers not only to evaluative research, although the profession will be obligated sooner or later to show empirical results, but to studying the phenomena themselves. For example, in any case situation regardless of the size of the unit of attention - the individual, family, groups, institution, or neighborhood - regardless of the configuration of the variables, what is the condition requiring attention? What are the circumstances creating the stress? What are the norms and the expectable goals? What are the patterns of problems? Why do some people function under stress and others do not? What are the models of competence in our society? What are the adaptive models of life, how can they be promoted through practice interventions, and what do developmental life tasks require of social services? If social work is to become task oriented, it will need a lot of interesting research to know what the tasks are. This will be one of the consequences of becoming a substantive profession in which methods and skills respond to need, rather than vice versa.

The third constraint implicit in the ecosystems orientation to practice is that as soon as social workers widen their perspective and take a contextual rather than methodological stance on practice, they will find that there is more to be done than they had noticed before. Perhaps the methods constriction was functional in maintaining their denial of what had to be done. No single methods formulation can take it all in. Social workers in agencies and social service facilities are finding out that the most refined clinical practice means little in the discharge process when there are limited institutional resources. A model of practice involving services over a nine-month period cannot be applied to a patient receiving services for only two days and a two-day model of practice will have to include other therapeutic resources beyond the treatment relationship. Accountability for a job to be done pushes social workers to notice things they were able to avoid before. The utilization of an ecomap, showing a client in his or her whole personal, social, cultural, and institutional field opens up potential for understanding his or her unique condition as well as possibilities for intervention. The more open social workers' understanding, the more open the interventive possibilities.[7] Perhaps the openness is what has frightened social workers; perhaps it is what has interested so many people in private practice. If this orientation forces social workers to confront the clients' complex reality, how are they to do their work? Perhaps their response to this enormous task has been to retreat to less threatening practice approaches.

The following chapters reflect and describe concepts and models of treatment which transcend the personal encounters of worker and client. They reflect an holistic interdisciplinary approach to therapeutic change. The approach within each setting, whether it be in a geriatric setting, a residential school or a community based facility is eclectic, but it also recognizes the importance of linkage to various agencies and systems. The problems inherent in certain models of treatment do not negate the need for fresh thinking or the inherent strengths in these models and concepts.

Current Trends in the Understanding of the Etiology of Criminal Behavior From a Bio-Psychosocial Perspective

Abstract: This paper is a theoretical description with some practical implications in the treatment of criminal and deviant behavior. It originated from my interest in understanding why so many individuals whom we treated at T.I.P. Neighborhood House were able to transcend their environment and experiences while others were affected adversely by these experiences and surroundings in the urban ghetto we know as the South Bronx.

The paper will attempt to show that violent deviant behavior is the result of biological as well as psychosocial variables. The indications are that the interaction of their variables upon the individual will bring about deviant and/or criminal behavior. Its impact on treatment, therefore, is quite significant in that it forces the social work practitioner to assess and treat the deviant individual from a holistic, interdisciplinary frame of reference.

Introduction: The social phenomenon of crime, as it exists in western society and particularly in the United States, has caused enormous consternation among its victims and potential victims and a great deal of research and money have been spent to understand its causes and how to prevent it. In the United States, it is a pervasive and continuous social ill which destroys hundreds of thousands of individuals each year, costs millions of dollars and is a threat to the very foundations of society. For example, in 1975, it was stated that there were twenty-one serious crimes committed in the United States every minute. It is estimated that there was a murder every twenty-six minutes, a woman forcibly raped every nine minutes, a robbery every sixty-eight seconds, a burglary every ten seconds, and a theft of $50.00 or more, every five seconds. In all likelihood these figures are underestimated, since not all crimes are reported.[1]

Social scientists and others have tried to assess the true incidence of criminal behavior in the population, as distinguished from the incidence shown by official reports. Almost all of these studies have shown that much more crime exists than is indicated by official reports. For instance, Jay R. Williams & Martin Gold studied the 847 adolescents surveyed in the 1967 National Survey of Youth to examine the differences between self-reported and "official" delinquency. They found that 83 percent had committed a chargeable offense within three years; less than 3 percent of the offenses were discovered by the police.[2] The National Opinion Research Center (NORC) surveyed 10,000 households in 1965 and concluded that the actual crime rate in the United States was about twice as great as the official crime rate. About half of those interviewed said that they had been victims of crimes they had not reported to the police.[3]

In 1974, the Law Enforcement Assistance Administration (LEAA) released the results of a sampling of about 200,000 citizens in eight cities. Because people do not always report them to the F.B.I., individuals were asked for their own experiences with crime. In general, the citizens reported about twice as much crime as official statistics show.[4] A second LEAA report comparing cities showed that the crime rate as reported by citizens was five times as high in Philadelphia as that shown by the F.B.I. reports, about three times as high in Chicago, Detroit, and Los Angeles, and twice as high in New York.[5]

These reports, however, are not conclusive. Although the NORC and LEAA studies were carefully conducted investigations and may be presumed to be generally accurate, we do not know the real state of affairs and perhaps never can in any detail. Statistics on crime rates are notoriously inaccurate, and conclusions based on them must be carefully assessed. Victimization studies, for example, may overreport criminal activity as a result of misunderstanding of the event, ignorance of the law, memory failure, interviewer error, and outright lying.[6] Nevertheless, there does seem to be more crime in the United States in recent years than in previous times, and it is clear that there is more crime than the official statistics show. We do not know, however, how much more there is nor all of the reasons behind the recent increase. Simple explanations should be suspected. There is a great deal more to the explanation of crime - or any other deviant behavior - than such popular explanations as moral breakdown, molly-coddling, permissiveness, and so forth.[7]

Biological factors: A revolution in our understanding of crime is quietly overthrowing some established doctrines. Until recently, criminologists looked for the causes of crime almost entirely in the offenders' social circumstances. There seemed to be no shortage of circumstances to blame: weakened, chaotic or broken families, ineffective schools, anti-social gangs, racism, poverty, unemployment.[8] Criminologists took seriously, more so than many other students of social behavior, the famous dictum of the French sociologist Emile Durkheim. "Social facts must have social explanations."[9] The sociological theory of crime had the unquestioned support of prominent editorialists, commentators, politicians and most thoughtful people.

Today, many learned journals and scholarly works draw a different picture. Sociological factors have not been abandoned, but increasingly it is becoming clear to many scholars that crime is the outcome of an interaction between social factors and certain biological factors, particularly for the offenders who, by repeated crimes, have made public places dangerous. The idea is still controversial, but increasingly, to the old question "Are Criminals Made or Born?" The answer seems to be both. The causes of crime lie in a combination of predisposing biological traits channeled by social circumstances into criminal behavior. The traits alone do not inevitably lead to crime; the circumstances do not make criminals of everyone; but together they create a population responsible for a large fraction of America's problem of crime in the streets.

Evidence that criminal behavior has deeper roots than social circumstances has always been right at hand, but social science has, until recent years, overlooked its implications. As far as the records show, crime everywhere and throughout history is disproportionately a young man's pursuit. Whether men are 20 or more times as likely to be arrested as women, as is the case in Malawi or Brunei, or only four to six times as likely, as in the United States or France, the sex difference in crime statistics is universal. Similarly, 18 year olds may sometimes be four times as likely to be criminals as 40 year olds, while at other times only twice as likely. In the United States, more than half of all arrests for serious property crimes are of 20 year olds or younger. Nowhere have older persons been as criminal as younger ones.[10]

Ultimately, the very universality of the age and sex difference in crime have alerted some social scientists to the implausibility of a theory that does not look beyond the accidents of particular societies. If cultures as different as Japan's and Sweden's, England's and Mexico's, have sex and age differences in crime then perhaps we should have suspected from the start that there was something more fundamental going on than parents happening to decide to raise their boys and girls differently. What is it about boys, girls and their parents, in societies of all sorts, that leads them to emphasize, rather than overcome, sex differences? Moreover, even if we believed that every society has arbitrarily decided to inculcate aggressiveness in males, there would still be the greater criminality among young males to explain. After all, in some cultures, young boys are not denied adult responsibilities but are kept out of school, put to work tilling the land and made to accept obligations to the society.

There is a great deal of evidence that much crime has an aggressive component. After reviewing the evidence on sex differences in aggression, researchers have concluded that aggression has a foundation that is at least in part biological. Only that conclusion can be drawn from data that show that the average man is more aggressive than the average woman in all known societies, that the sex difference is present in infancy well before evidence of sex role, socialization by adults, that similar sex differences turn up in many of our biological relatives - monkeys and apes. Human aggression has been directly tied to sex hormones, particularly male sex hormones, in experiments on athletes engaging in competitive sports and on prisoners known for violent or domineering behavior. No single line of evidence is decisive and each can be challenged, but all together they convinced specialists in the social sciences that the sexual conventions that assign males the aggressive roles have biological roots.[11] That is also the conclusion of most researchers about the developmental forces that make adolescence and young adulthood a time of risk for criminal and other deviant behavior. This is when powerful new drives awaken leading to frustrations that foster behavior unchecked by the internalized prohibitions of adulthood. The result is usually just youthful rowdiness, but, in a minority of cases, it passes over the line into crime.

Psychological factors: Freudian psychologists maintain that all people have deviant impulses toward sexuality and aggression, but that in the process of growing up most of us learn to inhibit them. Freud argued that through identification with their parents, children acquire a superego, or conscience, that forbids deviant kinds of behavior, and an ego that enables them to deal realistically with internal drives and social demands.[12] Psychoanalytic theory suggests that acts of wanton cruelty and crimes committed without apparent motives may indicate an underdeveloped superego. Conversely, an overdeveloped superego may also lead to deviance. People who are repulsed by their own urges may commit deviant acts to receive the punishment they feel they deserve for bating their parents or for having sexual fantasies, for example.[13]

Other psychologists argue that we simply learn from those around us. Albert Bandura and Richard H. Walters, for example, compared groups of delinquent and non-delinquent white boys from financially stable homes. They found that continuously harsh physical discipline or overindulgence could lead to delinquency. Boys whose fathers often beat them tended to rely on external controls. They based decisions on the chances of being caught, not on inner feelings of right and wrong. On the other hand, boys who had their parents' uncritical approval grew up believing that anything they wanted to do was good - an assumption not always shared by the outside world.[14]

Despite the occasional assertion of mental health specialists to the contrary, there is little empirical evidence that any specific personality trait is associated with deviant behavior. No consistent psychological differences of any kind have been found to differentiate identified deviants from non-deviants. An overwhelming number of studies have shown that criminals and delinquents, at least, do not differ from the normal population in such matters as intelligence, frequency of feeblemindedness, personality test scores, or neurosis and psychosis.[15]

<u>Social factors</u>: This accumulation of negative evidence does not surprise sociologists. The psychoanalytic approach is based on the wrong assumption that deviants are different. Prison populations in the United States do differ significantly from the noninstitutionalized population. As a class, institutionalized criminals and delinquents are generally poorer and less educated than the rest of the population; they are less likely to be white, well educated, or from the middle or upper class. However, these differences are largely reflections of police practice, the judicial process, and cultural definitions of deviance. It should be noted that although nearly everyone violates the law, very few go to prison for it.

According to Tarvis Hirschi,

"Three fundamental perspectives on delinquency and deviant behavior dominate the current sociological scene. According to stress or motivational theories, legitimate desires that conformity cannot satisfy force a person into deviance. According to <u>control</u> or bond theories, a person is free to commit delinquent acts because his ties to the conventional order have somehow been broken. According to <u>cultural deviance</u> theories, the deviant conforms to a set of standards not accepted by a larger or more powerful society. Although most current theories of crime and delinquency contain elements of at least two and occasionally all three of these perceptions, reconciliation of the assumptions is very difficult."[16]

We will discuss each of these as types and describe some of the sociological approaches to deviance that exemplify them.

<u>Theories of Social Stress</u>: The essence of stress or strain theories is the assumption that when conformity to social norms fails to satisfy a person's legitimate desires, that person will eventually be forced to seek satisfaction through deviant means.[17] The concept of <u>anomie,</u> a state of deregulation or normlessness experienced

when there is no meaning or stability in life because of sudden depression, prosperity, or rapid technological change, was originally proposed by Emile Durkheim to explain certain forms of suicide.[18] Durkheim saw the aspirations of humans as having no limits, he thought that the collective order of norms and values established by society regulates human desires and keeps them within the bounds of realistic possibility.[19]

Robert K. Merton applied the concept of anomie in an American context as he sought to describe the different ways in which people adapt to the discrepancy between expectations and opportunities. He used stress theory to account for varying crime rates in different classes and linked high rates of deviance to anomie.[20] For example, people may expect to have a job, but the economy may not provide enough jobs to go around. Merton reasoned that to some degree all people internalize the goals considered worth striving for in their culture. Everyone also internalizes the norms governing proper and legitimate ways of striving for these goals. When opportunities for achieving highly valued goals, as the culture defines them, do not exist people seek alternatives. Thus, "some social structures exert a definite pressure upon certain persons in the society to engage in nonconforming rather than in conforming behavior."[21]

Merton defined conformity as seeking culturally approved goals by culturally approved means. He outlined four types of deviant behavior that may occur when social realities do not match cultural expectations. One type is <u>innovation</u> - pursuing culturally approved goals by deviant means. A thief, for example, is pursuing the same objective as a working person namely, money, the things it can buy, and the advantage it confers. Another way to resolve conflicts between goals and means is <u>ritualism</u>, adhering rigidly to norms at the expense of goals. A teacher who maintains order in the classroom and delivers lessons in the prescribed way regardless of whether students learn anything is a ritualist. Merton uses the term retreatism to describe giving up. Retreatists are people who have lost the desire to pursue certain cultural goals as well as the belief that following certain norms is intrinsically worthwhile. Retreatists are the bohemians, beatniks, hippies, alcoholics, and drug addicts, and psychotics who are alienated from society. Finally, people who are alienated from both the goals and the standards of their culture may come up with new ideals and new rules for pursuing them. Merton calls this rebellion. The Weatherman and the short-lived Symbionese Liberation Army are examples.[22]

Anomie theory helps us understand the relationship between poverty and crime. In other societies the demand for financial success is not the same for all social classes. All are not created equal in India, Italy, or England. In most of the world, children of the ghetto are not expected to "rise above," but rather to make do as best they can with what is available to them.[23] In the United States, all men and women are supposed to be equal, and thus all Americans are expected to gain economic affluence. We are held personally responsible if we do not. The goal is the same for all, despite racism, homophobia, sexism, overt and covert class structures that exist. Thus, if money cannot be made through legitimate means, non-legitimate means often come to be used.

Cultural Transmission of Deviance: In the 1920's, Clifford Shaw and Henry McKay noted that high crime rates had persisted in the same Chicago neighborhood for over twenty years, even though different ethnic groups had come and gone. Obviously, ethnic traditions could not explain the crime rate. In one of the classic studies of deviance and criminal behavior, Shaw & McKay found that newcomers were continuously learning deviant ways from established residents, primarily in playgroups and teenage groups.[24] Once the newcomers had absorbed the neighborhood norms and values, they in turn passed them on to the next wave of immigrants.

Shaw & McKay's study was supported by the work of Edwin Sutherland, whose Principles of Criminology contain an explanation of how this cultural transmission - the process by which deviance is learned through the transmission of norms within a community or group take place. Its assumption is that criminal behavior is learned through association with others. It is neither physiological nor inherited, nor the product of warped psychology.[25]

If criminal behavior is learned as any other behavior is learned, then it is learned through association with others, especially interaction within intimate personal groups. Throughout our lives, association and interaction with others teach us motives, attitudes, values, and rationalizations. The specific direction that these will take - law abiding or law-violative - will depend on from whom we learn our behavior. Thus, differential association - differences in with whom we associate - in large part determine how we behave.

Through the transmission of norms within a community or group, people can be socialized to the drug subculture, the homosexual subculture, the radical subculture, the criminal subculture, and so forth. For just as some communities offer young people opportunities for education, role models of people who have achieved success by conventional means, and contacts with people who can help advance their careers, other communities offer opportunities for learning how to hustle and evade authorities, role models of people who have achieved success as gamblers or pimps, and contacts with the underworld.[26] For example, in New York and Harlem, thousands of street wise youngsters between the ages of nine and seventeen are exploited and manipulated by being told that they can make a lot of money simply by selling little envelopes of heroin and cocaine which they are given by drug dealers. The inducements to become a "runner" are strong, by the time he was fifteen, one "runner" had earned himself enough money to buy a $12,000 car. The deterrents, on the other hand, are too often comparatively weak. As one young girl told a reporter, "I was spending the money to help my family. Mom didn't care if I ever went back to school, so long as I brought in the money."[27]

Community norms and values have as strong an effect on youths growing up in a high-crime neighborhood as on youths being raised in conventional ones. Walter Miller, who did a three year participant-observational study, called these norms "focal concerns." For lower-class urban adolescent males, Miller found they included trouble with the law and with women; toughness includes physical prowess and playing it cool; smartness is being able to outsmart and con others, as well as a respect for verbal quickness and ingenuity; fate entails a sense that many forces are beyond one's control, that success is a matter of luck, and autonomy which relates to a resentment of outside controls. Such delinquent acts as drinking or stealing cars, Miller concluded, are expressions of these important subcultural concerns; delinquency, he argued, can thus be seen as "a directed attempt ... to adhere to forms of behavior and to achieve standards as they are defined in that community."[28]

Edwin Sutherland maintains that people may become delinquent or deviant to the degree that they associate and interact with others who favor law violation more commonly than they oppose it. Such association varies in frequency, duration, intensity, and priority, and these variables determine what individuals learn or how well they learn it. Further, while criminal behavior is an expression of general needs and values in the psychoanalytic sense, it cannot be explained by such things, i.e. aggressiveness, because non-criminal behavior is an expression of the same needs and values. It is not "need for money" that explains criminality, but the choices that an individual makes to fulfill that need. Such choices are the product of life-long learning - and interaction with others.[29]

Social-bond Theory: The two theories that we have examined so far both assume that people want to conform, according to stress theory, people try first to conform to the normal pattern achieving success, and turn to illegitimate means only after the legitimate approaches have failed. Cultural transmission theorists argue that even deviants conform, but that they conform to the norms of a deviant community or subculture. Social bond theory, in contrast, is built on the assumption that people are in conflict with social norms.[30] According to this theory, when people do conform, it's only because they are forced to do so by social bonds. When their bonds weaken or dissolve, people are apt to become deviant, disoriented, or suicidal.

Some strong support for social-bond theory comes from the comprehensive study of delinquency conducted by Travis Hirschi. The data in this study did not support the notion that deviance springs from the pressure of unfulfilled but legitimate desires, or from subcultural or group traditions and relationships. Rather, when Hirschi compared delinquents to nondelinquents, he found that delinquents were less attached to family, friends, or conventional goals. The delinquent, Hirschi concluded, was best described as "a person relatively free of the intimate attachments, the aspirations, and the moral beliefs that bind the law."[31] The weakness of social bonds, in other words, appeared to be the most conspicuous factor behind delinquent behavior.

Each of the sociological theories of deviance and criminology offers valid insights into a phenomenon involving a wide range of forms, contexts and social groupings. These insights are not mutually exclusive: the pressure that society places on its members to succeed; the role that a group can play in giving an individual a sense of identity; and the control that social rules and conventions can have over social action may all contribute to the rate of deviance in a group.

<u>Significance of Findings</u>: When we look at the causes of crime from various perspectives we realize the complexity of the problem. There are many theories which make sense and which are questionable. It seems that there are many variables which ultimately foreshadow criminal and deviant behavior. Variables must conclude biological as well as psychosociological ones. The indications are that the interdependence and interaction of these variables upon the individual will bring about deviant and/or criminal behavior.

Traits that foreshadow serious recurrent criminal behavior have been traced all the way back to behavior patterns such as hyperactivity and unusual fussiness, and neurological origins such as atypical brain waves or reflexes. In at least a minority of cases, these are detectable in the first few years of life. Some of the characteristics are sex linked. There is evidence that newborn females are more likely than newborn males to smile, to cling to their mothers, to be receptive to touching and talking, to be receptive to certain stimuli, such as being touched by a cloth and to have less upper body strength. Mothers certainly treat girls and boys differently, but the differences are not simply a matter of the mother's choice - female babies are more responsive than male babies to precisely the kind of treatment that is regarded as "feminine."[32] When adults are asked to play with infants, they play with them in ways they think are appropriate to the infants' sexes. However, there is also some evidence that when the sex of the infant is concealed, the behavior of the adults is influenced by the conduct of the child.

Premature infants or those born with low birth weights have a special problem. These children are vulnerable to any adverse circumstances in their environment, including child abuse, that may foster crime. Although nurturing parents can compensate for adversity, cold or inconsistent parents may exacerbate it. Prematurity and low birth weight may result from poor prenatal care, a bad diet or excessive use of alcohol or drugs. Whether the bad care is due to poverty, ignorance or anything else here we see criminality rising from biological, though not necessarily genetic, factors. It is now known that these babies are more likely than normal babies to be the victims of child abuse.[33]

This is not to blame child abuse on the victims, but, unless parents are emotionally prepared for the task of caring for such children, they may vent their frustration at the infant's unresponsiveness by hitting or neglecting it. Whatever it is in parent and child that leads to prematurity or low birth weight is compounded by the subsequent action between them.[34]

The etiology of criminal behavior and the problems of crime and deviant behavior are complex and varied and troubling. We currently recognize that chronic offenders typically begin their misconduct at an early age. Early family and preschool programs may be far better resources for the crime prevention dollar than so-called rehabilitation programs aimed, usually futilely, at the 19 or 20 year old veteran offender. Prevention programs risk stigmatizing children, but this may be less of a risk than neglect. If stigma were a problem to be avoided at all costs, we would have to dismantle most special needs education programs.[35]

Above all there is a case for redirecting research into the cause of crime in ways that take into account the interaction of biological and psychosocial factors. Some researchers are exploring these issues by analyzing social and biological information from large groups as they age from infancy to adulthood and linking the data to criminal behavior. However, much more needs to be done. The causes and problems of criminal behavior as it presents itself to our society, poses a massive challenge to social scientists, biologists, and practitioners. It currently appears to underscore the need for a multidisciplinary approach.

Social workers, to whom essentially this Independent Study Project is addressed, cannot operate alone. The worker is linked to two significant foci: the social agency and the client. Each is linked to each other in specific ways. The worker is linked to the agency by the roles he or she plays within the agency. The agency is linked to the worker through a job description and some form of contractual agreement. The client is linked to the worker by how he or she responds to the worker. The agency is linked to the client by how it delivers services, and the client is linked to the agency through how she or he uses the services offered.

This relationship does not take place in a vacuum. It takes place in both community and societal contexts. The values and structure of the community and society determine the context of the human service activity. It is therefore imperative that the social service agency develop linkages with other resources such as medical, educational and employment to contain and structure the individual client whose behavior is antisocial and/or criminal in the eyes of the community.

According to Lewis Robbins, "Human beings, society and man and his total environment are functioning wholes in nature with unique attributes that cannot be understood by analysis of the parts alone. New approaches are needed to emphasize the holistic nature of man and of the systems - biological, psychological, and social - of which he is an integral part."[36]

The promise of a therapeutic approach which is holistic or epidemiological is that one can gain a powerful perspective on the relationship between persons, groups, communities and societies; how they interrelate, and how to work for change via manipulation of these interrelations.[37]

CHAPTER III

Developing a Domestic Violence Model in a Community Based Agency in the South Bronx

Abstract: This paper is based on a project which I developed and administered at Tremont Improvement Program (TIP) Neighborhood House. We were able to obtain funds from the New York State Department of Social Services for the fiscal year of October '84 through September '85 based on a concept and treatment model which I had written in April '84.

This paper embellishes on the original material sent to the Department of Social Services. Its emphasis is on direct services for battered spouses. It maintains that the social worker's understanding of the dynamics of domestic violence should be based on a psychosocial framework, not merely on traditional Freudian psychotherapeutic principles. Counseling with battered women can be most effective when it is a short-term process focused on problem solving.

Introduction: Spouse abuse is usually known as wife abuse in that most reported victims tend to be female and most batterers tend to be male. This abuse has been recognized as a social problem only in recent years. The practice has existed throughout history, however, and was sanctioned until late in the last century by laws governing a man's right to control his property. Although these laws no longer exist, the physical abuse of women by the men with whom they have intimate relationships continues to be covertly and, at times, overtly sanctioned by society.[1]

A decade ago, virtually no literature existed on the subject of spouse abuse except for psychiatrically oriented discussions of sadomasochistic marital relationships.[2] Today, however, sociological literature emphasizing the social nature of spouse abuse is beginning to accumulate. In addition, a body of clinically oriented social work literature developed in the 1970's with an emphasis on the characteristics of the victim and his/her abuser and with recommendations for appropriate agency policies and interventive strategies on the victim's behalf. In both the sociological and social work literatures, authors tend to use a general systems theory approach to the problem among family members and to emphasize structural factors that make violence a possibility in all families. Complementing and serving as an impetus for academic and clinical research is a vigorous feminist literature embodying the innovative ideas and passionate commitment that have characterized this movement.

The movement to defend women against physical abuse has arisen at a time in history when the conditions that are being deplored are probably less widespread than they were in earlier times when lower expectations prevailed. However, one general factor and two specific factors combined in the decade of the 1970's to lift the problem of wife abuse out of obscurity. The general factor, a rise in the second half of the twentieth century of a strong belief throughout the society in greater equality for all groups, created a milieu that was sympathetic to the plight of victims, including abused wives. In this milieu, the groundwork was laid by publicity given to two other problems that had been recently discovered: child abuse and rape. This publicity forced public acknowledgement that beneath the orderly surface of many families, lay a substratum of domestic violence that permeated all layers of the society.[3]

In the South Bronx, there is an enormous need for services within the area of domestic violence. While statistics are not clear, somewhat vague and perhaps subjective, it is the opinion of professionals that the following is true:

1) Almost 100% of the victims of domestic violence are female.
2) Within community districts 1, 2 and 3, 60% to 70% of families residing in these districts have experienced domestic violence.
3) Within community districts 4, 5 and 6, it is estimated that between 30% to 40% of families residing there have experienced domestic violence.

Development of a Domestic Violence Project: The community-based agency, Tremont Improvement Program (TIP) Neighborhood House, with which I have been associated for the past 5 years, is located in district 6. Staff estimates that these figures, while high, may not even convey the actual figures in relation to domestic violence. Despite these incredible figures, delivery service systems are few and far between. In the South Bronx in which TIP is located, there are only two shelters available for battered wives. There is one educational program for batterers and there is but one agency which provides comprehensive services for families in the throes of domestic violence -- Fordham Tremont Community Mental Health Center -- which is outside of community district 6.

In community district 6, there are no agencies, except for TIP, which provides comprehensive services to meet the problem of domestic violence. A needs assessment which was completed in February 1981 revealed that the population of district 6 is primarily young, especially between the cohorts of 5-12 through 25-44 years of age.[4] Among the specific problems which relate to this population and which is compounded by socioeconomic stress is the problem of domestic violence. Since TIP is a community based, non-profit agency, it applied for funding in May '84 and was approved for funding in August '84.

The Applicant Organization

Tremont Improvement Program (TIP) Neighborhood House, Inc. was established in 1972 as a store front program to help meet the critical need for social services in the Bronx Park South-East Tremont Community, an area characterized by severe poverty, a high incidence of crime, streets crowded with unemployed youth and adults, unwed mothers and a landscape studded with deteriorated and abandoned buildings.[5] Financial backing was provided by Phipps Houses, the non-profit sponsor of several hundred units of low income housing constructed in the South Bronx in the early 1970's. Since that modest beginning, only 13 years ago, TIP has evolved into a multifaceted community service organization whose target area has broadened to include the entire borough of the Bronx.

TIP's Family Services, prior to the funding for domestic violence, had served more than 189 families annually through counseling and delinquency diversion and focused on those aspects of family living where interpersonal relationships create problems that endanger the well-being of family members. The primary objectives of TIP's Family Services have been to identify families at risk and provide them with services which prevent their children from being institutionalized, or in cases in which children are institutionalized, hasten their return to their families and communities.

Through individual family counseling, families have interfaced with an interdisciplinary team of trained social workers, paraprofessionals and community volunteers. Direct services such as day care, home management, recreation and emergency assistance are provided. In addition, the formation of a Parents Anonymous group and a single adolescent mothers group serve as resources to the families themselves. Community mental health facilities, the Department of Social Services, District Advisory Councils and other agencies and resources provide a network of support to these families.

It was the Family Services Unit of TIP which was designed to administer and implement the Domestic Violence Project in that the unit had a good track record in delivering mental health services and counseling to individuals and families in the Bronx. The staff had also helped, among others, victims of domestic violence and/or spouse abuse and had been able to make appropriate referrals when necessary. In addition the agency had been able to help develop supportive networks with other community agencies as well. In effect, it had the staff and the funding sources to develop an effective program in the area of domestic violence.

Project Objectives and Goals: The project was set up to utilize a comprehensive approach to the problem of domestic violence. We proposed a plan for treating couples and for families in which battering is either the presenting problem or is revealed at some point in therapy. The main objectives of this model were as follows:

1) Case finding or assessment of the problem and history of the relationship.
2) Case management which reflects an advocacy approach.
3) Therapy and ongoing counseling.
4) Community education.

The goals of this project were as follows:

1) To make a range of comprehensive services available to families which have experienced domestic violence and victims of spouse abuse.

2) To join the local network of service providers.
3) To provide community education and outreach in underserved areas of the community.

Casefinding or Assessment

Victims of domestic violence have been referred to TIP by Crime Victims Services, Family Court, police precincts, community mental health centers and other community resources and facilities. The population which is served are those individuals and families who have suffered the trauma of spouse abuse. This client population suffers the trauma of spouse abuse and resides in the neighborhood communities which TIP serves. Its composition is both male and female and consists of multi-ethnic and racial components. Intake, advocacy, and ongoing counseling is done by caseworkers. The first phase of treatment is usually accomplished with the batterer and battered spouse separately in order to expedite the information-gathering process. Separate therapy serves to minimize the risk of additional violence and maximize the atmosphere for each spouse to provide the "whole truth". The use of a female caseworker to interview the woman and a male to interview the man also reduces resistance and increases the opportunity for communicating acceptance in the face of the client's embarrassment, doubt, fear and anger.

According to Costantino, "... The initial part of the intake interview should be devoted to fact gathering. This gives structure and limits to the session and allows the interviewer to assess both the problem and the client. Data gathered from the client should include information on identity, employment, education, living arrangements, criminal history, probation or parole status of the client and the batterer, history of the couple's relationships, names and ages of children (if any), incidents and patterns of violence, effects of the violence on any children and on the client herself, and the type of assistance that the client is requesting from the unit..."[6]

The second part of the interview should involve an attempt to educate the client. Basic survival skills and legal rights should be taught; printed handouts containing such information should be given to every client for reference. Costantino goes on to state as follows: "... Clients should be taught how to deal effectively with the police, including what to say when calling for assistance, the importance of recording the officers' names and badge numbers, the procedure for filing a police report, and the need to collect and save evidence. It may be helpful to engage the client in a role-play situation and have her act out a mock contact with the police. The process for making a citizen's arrest should be discussed, as should information on pursuing criminal charges or civil remedies...."[7]

The third part of the intake interview is client ventilation, or the process of allowing the client to express her fears, anger, and ambivalence. "However ... the initial interview is not meant to be a counseling session even though a certain amount of crisis intervention may be necessary."[8]

Finally, an intervention plan is to be formulated. At the end of the interview, the client is to have a clear understanding of what is being done with her case, what her responsibilities are as a client, and whether or not the unit will be legally representing her or active only from a social work perspective.

In addition to questions about how long the battering has been going on, its severity, and when the most recent incident occurred, it's important for the therapist to find out what happened just before the last acute incident and immediately after it in order to begin to focus on a sequence of events which may reveal a pattern. It helps to get as much detail as possible from the stories of the batterer and battered spouse. What they each typically say and how they believe in their cycle of violence give clues, not only about the issues involved, but to the purpose which the violence serves in their relationship. Assessment of the severity of violence is done in individual interviews with each spouse. In deciding whether to stress individual or conjoint therapy, the severity of violence, the amount of verbal fighting that occurs during the conjoint sessions, and the spouses' ambivalence about maintaining the marriage are considered. If violence is severe and life threatening, each spouse is seen separately as information from the therapy sessions may escalate tensions and increase the potential for another violent episode. Ambivalence toward maintaining a chaotic marriage is viewed as a healthy sign and is an indicator that both partners may be ready for individual therapy or separate groups.

Case Management: Costantino states:

"... The purpose of social work services is to assist the battered woman with her psychosocial problems during the crisis period of domestic violence..."[9]

At TIP, the victim might be encouraged to leave the perpetrator and utilize various direct services. These services would include the following:

1) Setting up a hot line system for victims. TIP's Domestic Violence Project provides crisis counseling and referrals over the telephone. The caseworker will, when necessary, encourage clients to utilize the toll free 800 hotline that can provide these services when the project office is closed.
2) Obtaining temporary shelter for victim and children.
3) Court referrals to obtain an order of protection.
4) Advocacy services such as housing assistance, public assistance, and legal assistance.

At TIP, the individual and/or family is able to obtain an array of services depending on the degree and extent of domestic violence.

The caseworker helps the battered spouse make detailed plans for her protection. She may need assistance in any of the following ways:

1) Identifying cues that warn of the imminence of another battering incident.
2) Deciding whom she will call or notify.
3) Determining how she will get out and what she will take with her.
4) Informing her of supportive community services, groups and organizations.

Unless the batterer has already made a commitment to nonviolence, the caseworker needs, in addition to helping design a protection plan, to confront the battered spouse about the improbability of the relationship changing unless she is willing to leave. Going for counseling is usually not enough to interrupt the cycle; therefore, the caseworker needs to convey hopelessness for change in the face of their recurrent cycle. Separation can give the couple the necessary breathing room to begin to change their "rules" and their pattern, but the separation usually is not sufficient to break the symbolistic tendencies of the couple. The separation has to be initiated by the battered spouse, who is in physical danger if she stays. Like the spouse of an alcoholic, she is generally the "overadequate" one and therefore able to provide the leverage in the relationship system. However, their mutual dependency needs preclude a decision to separate unless she is "hitting bottom" and can take no more in the relationship. If she decides she is ready to do so, the caseworker's responsibility is to help her focus on herself and not on expecting her partner to change.[10]

The program at TIP does not exclude families in which the batterer is not involved in counseling. Advocacy and direct counseling for the victims are of paramount importance. The goals are to help the victim assess her situation, determine what actions are necessary to provide immediate safety for herself and her children, and help her determine what longer term actions and service are necessary to provide for the safety, well-being and support of herself and her children. In addition, workers are encouraged and indeed expected to run support groups for the victims and for the children from violent homes.

Workers provide the victims of abuse and domestic violence advocacy services for hard to obtain services such as housing, food stamps, public assistance, the legal system. TIP's Domestic Violence Project is in a very good position to maintain linkage with over 100 agencies throughout the Bronx. TIP has very close working relationships with such agencies as Fordham Tremont Community Mental Health Center, Montefiore Hospital, Crime Victims Services, North Bronx Central Hospital, Crotona Park Community Mental Health Center, University Consultation Center, among others. TIP is involved in various network and linkage systems such as Preventive Association of Community Agencies (PRACA), the Bronx Task Force on Child Abuse and Neglect, the Bronx Teen Pregnancy Network. Thus referrals are made to and from a large number of agencies when needed. An example of this is Fordham Tremont Community Mental Health Center which has an educational program for male batterers. An agreement was worked out with FTCMHC that TIP is available to sponsor a self-help group for those male batterers who wish to continue in a group subsequent to their involvement in the Domestic Violence Program at Fordham Tremont Community Mental Health Center.

Therapy and Ongoing Counseling

If a male/female co-casework team is implementing the treatment, the "agreement" for the batterer may occur simultaneously with the protection plan for the battered spouse. Motivation can be a difficult aspect of the therapy with the batterer. It helps to support his strength and courage for coming in and to let him know he can learn how to not be controlled by someone else. The caseworker urges a non-violence agreement, written if possible, from the batterer as early in the treatment as possible. The batterer is encouraged to develop and use a support network at times of crisis. The caseworker can explain that his battering may be very similar to drug addiction and as a learned response to stress, can be "treated."[11]

Groups, if available, ideally can provide support for changes, identification with others struggling with similar problems and education in the effects of patriarchal values in our society, as well as assertiveness training and anger management training. If group therapy is not possible, the move toward independence in the form of depression, stress and anger management, to adoption of more assertive lifestyles can be encouraged in individual therapy.[12] When the risk of violence has been significantly reduced through work in the above areas, the caseworker can bring the couple together for continual work in such areas as negotiation from an equal perspective, communication skills, recognition of each other's cues of anger and development of alternatives to violence.

Community Education: At TIP, caseworkers, in addition to counseling and referring to other community services, provides community education to public and community agencies concerning the identity and treatment of abused spouses and their batterers. Workshops are held to train staff of various local agencies, police precincts, and medical centers. Guest speakers are invited and can utilize films, cassettes, and slides to enhance presentations.

Conclusion: TIP's Domestic Violence Project is a model whose main objectives are as follows:

1) Case finding or assessment of the problem and history of the relationship.

2) Case management which reflects an advocacy approach.
3) Therapy and ongoing counseling.
4) Community education.

The social worker's understanding of the dynamics of domestic violence should be based on a psychosocial framework, not merely on traditional Freudian psychotherapeutic principles. Counseling with battered women can be most effective when it is a short-term process focused on problem solving. A battered woman needs to set goals, develop and experience self-confidence, and measure her progress. Counseling should thus be a time-limited, goal-specific activity.[13] Victims of domestic violence, if they are to make the changes necessary to leave an abusive situation, require a great amount of time and support. On the other hand, according to Bonnie Carlson,

"... Victims who choose to stay in their situation and hope to improve it also need support. But if the assailant's environment, either external or internal, does not change in a meaningful way, the prognosis for the improvement of the victim's situation is not favorable."[14]

As long as men believe that responding to stress and frustration with aggression or physical violence is acceptable behavior, the problem of the battered wife will continue to exist. Thus, in addition to improving the ability of men and women to support themselves and their families, efforts should be made to eradicate the beliefs that (1) men's status must and should be higher than women's; (2) men who are not dominant and are not physically more powerful than women are in some way not masculine and not adequate; and (3) physical power and coercion are valid means of solving disputes in the family or in any other interpersonal relationships.[15] Until these fundamental changes in attitude have become widely accepted, helping professionals must try to reach out to a victimized population too long ignored. They must recognize that battered women are not women who are mentally ill, but rather are troubled women in need of emotional support as well as tangible assistance.

CHAPTER IV

A Concept Paper on a Parent Training and Self Help Program at TIP Neighborhood Home

Abstract: During the last year that I remained at TIP as Director of Family Services, we had an opportunity to review a contract with Greater New York Fund for $60,000. This was predicated on our ability to emphasize parent training in relation to helping parents to become more effective with their children. Our primary goal was to reduce the potential for child abuse.

What I have done here is to expand the concept paper so that it includes footnotes and a bibliography. Its original contents essentially remain the same.

This concept paper was sent to Ms. Barbara Coleman who was the liaison person at Greater New York Fund and who, in the past, enabled us to obtain monies from the agency for our family service program at TIP.

The concept paper was approved to enable us to obtain a new contract for $30,000 from the Greater New York Fund.

Introduction: A major emphasis in TIP's Family Services Unit will be on parent education. We hope to expand and strengthen our current Parents Anonymous self-help group, our teen mothers education group and develop a program, in conjunction with other agencies, i.e. the Bronx Task Force on Child Abuse and Neglect, to develop a training program for parents who in turn will become trainers in the area of parent-child relations and parent management. The body of knowledge to be applied will be derived from our understanding of human behavior and Parents Effectiveness Training (P.E.T.) techniques which were developed by Thomas Gordon.[1] Social workers, psychologists and psychiatrists have long recognized that the parent-child relationship is crucial to a child's present and future mental health. The primary responsibility of parents is to facilitate their child in physical and emotional development, and yet what constitutes the facilitation of emotional development in particular has been a nebulous and controversial subject.

As an extension of his work in psychotherapy, Rogers proposed that people who facilitate emotional growth are those who communicate with empathic understanding, warmth and genuineness.[2] Similarly, research evidence suggests that therapists who offer high levels of empathy, warmth, and genuineness encourage positive change in their clients, whereas low levels of these conditions are factors in clients' deterioration. In addition, there is also evidence that therapists and lay people can be trained to communicate more responsively. A number of programs have been developed in the past several years to train therapists, teachers, parents and others to be more facilitative in their interpersonal relationships. Empirical research on these programs is scarce, however.

Parent Effectiveness Training (P.E.T.) is one such training program available nationwide. P.E.T. is a systematically designed training course in which an instructor meets with a group of parents who want to learn and practice interpersonal and problem-solving skills to improve their relationship with their children. The group meets for a three-hour workshop once a week for a period of eight weeks, a total of 24 hours of training. The class size is from ten to twenty people. The course uses various instructional methods, including brief lectures, tape recordings, role-playing, role-modeling, a textbook, and a workbook. Instructors are trained and licensed.[3]

At TIP, we would plan, in cooperation with other community based preventive programs, to allow social workers to receive P.E.T. training. They in turn would provide P.E.T. training to selected parents who in turn would act as parent trainers for other parents in the community. Hopefully, this parent training program would have a pyramid effect on the community with large numbers of parents both training and receiving training in parent-child relations.

"The influence that parents have on their children's emotional development is undisputed."[4] Training for parenthood is sadly lacking, however, and has been assumed to be unnecessary. Yet studies have shown that few people in our society have skills that foster and nurture positive emotional growth.[5] The myth that parenting skills are somehow natural, instinctive and magically available serves to stigmatize those who seek such training. Although empathy, warmth and genuineness are not sufficient conditions for trouble free parenthood, the struggle for both children and parents could be eased perhaps if training were readily available.[6] P.E.T. shows potential value as a preventive measure to help parents become better facilitators of their children's emotional growth.

In addition to the above, we plan to expand and strengthen two existing programs within Family Services at TIP. They are the Parents Anonymous self-help group and the teen mothers group, both of which meet on a weekly basis. Both groups are educationally oriented and have reached a sizable number of parents. Parents Anonymous is geared to help abusive or potentially abusive parents from physically and emotionally harming their children. The teen mothers group is geared to educate parents in a wide range of areas from parent-child relations to nutrition. There is a focus on pre-natal and neo-natal phenomena as well.

Currently the leadership of Parents Anonymous (P.A.) at TIP is given by the Director of Family Services who acts as both group leader and sponsor. The leadership for the Teen Mother's group is provided by a parenting surrogate who has had life experience as a teen mother when she turned 17. Within P.A., the sponsor is attempting to get one of the group members to take over the leadership of the group. This is based on the premise that professionals might at times do better to recognize troubled parents as colleagues rather than as service recipients.

We believe at TIP that professionals can move beyond their traditional commitment to help people help themselves and become personally involved with their clients' causes and concerns. "This can best be done by learning how to remove the barriers to authentic human interaction that often exist between the helper and the helped."[7] Professionals may need to recognize that, in some instances, it may be as important to feel with their clients. This idea is beginning to be accepted in work with such groups as drug addicts and abusive parents.

Social workers at TIP will learn how to share their own personal concerns with clients, when appropriate, to experience what the client can give as well as receive. Professional interest in self-awareness, empathy, and support needs to be supplemented by learning experiences that teach openness, self-disclosure, and effective confrontation.[8]

There are hazards in carrying out these innovations. Staff may lose some of its professional perspective, objectivity, and authority. Nonetheless, the possibilities for increasing its usefulness to clients in their own helping efforts seem worth the risk.

CHAPTER V

Preliminary Report on TIP's Family Care Project

Abstract: In October 1980, I was employed at Tremont Improvement Program (TIP) Neighborhood House as a consultant. TIP is a community based agency in the South Bronx where there are many severe socio-economic problems. At the time in which I became part of the staff, TIP did not have a family service unit, despite the myriad problems of the community; i.e., high teen pregnancy rate, many reports of child abuse and familial dysfunction, etc. Then I was requested by the Executive Director, Mr. Hugh Haywood, to research, develop and write a needs assessment concerning Community District 6, the district in which TIP is located.

Subsequently, with the assistance of a colleague, Mr. Willis Kettrell, we completed a needs assessment in March 1981. The data and statistics, which were accumulated with a great deal of effort, were given to the Executive Director who subsequently presented the material to the Board of Directors. They approved it and gave permission for TIP to add Family Services to its existing services in April 1981.

Subsequently, I became the Project Director of Family Services. In essence, I became "chief cook and bottle washer." I counseled clients, maintained the files, went to interagency meetings, I did whatever I could do to keep the program viable.

As a result of this effort, in October '81, TIP received funding from the New York State Department of Social Services for one year. This occurred after I sent in a request for funding (RFP) by utilizing the State grant proposal form. The approved funding was for preventive purposes. The goal which was mandated by the state was for TIP to "identify families at risk and provide them with appropriate preventive services that would foster stability, prevent institutionalization of children or, in cases where children are institutionalized, hasten their return to the home and community." I was now able to hire staff and absorb social work students whom I subsequently supervised.

The following is a preliminary report which was ultimately approved by the State Consultant, Ms. Renee Gibson, subsequent to nine (9) months into the Family Care or Family Services Project. As a result of this report, we obtained additional funds for another 3 months of service. With assistance from private resources and other public services, TIP's Family Services Project survived and eventually in June 1984, TIP's Family Services was given funding approval by New York City's Special Services for Children for fiscal year October 1984 through September 1985.

The following report reveals that TIP's Family Care Project successfully met its goal which was to prevent children from going into Foster Care while supporting them and their families.

The report was done according to guidelines set by the New York State Department of Social Services. It included an outline page, a Table of Contents, a narrative, and various appendices which reflect the efforts made during the '81-'82 fiscal year to develop a comprehensive, viable program. For purposes of this I.S.P. I am excluding from the following the outline page and the Table of Contents.

Introduction:

I.   Background and Statement of the Problem: Tremont Improvement Program (TIP) Neighborhood House, Inc. is located in Community Planning Board #6. TIP's immediate target area, the West Farms-East Tremont section of the South Bronx, is populated primarily by Blacks 51% and Hispanic 48%, totalling more than 28,000 persons. This enormous concentration of people in our target area is underserved by health, social and other services.[1] In particular the Hispanic Community is almost invisible to traditional services where language and cultural barriers often serve as inhibiting factors. With specific respect to family consultations to families at risk and after-care services to institutionalized children, Child Welfare Information Services (C.W.I.S.) computerized zip code data indicate six hundred families living in our zip code 10460 and the contiguous areas - 10458, 10462, etc. have children in care.[2] In addition, Community Planning Board #6 and TIP's immediate target area have one of the highest infant mortality rates in the city and state with more than 27 per thousand. Among the contributing factors are teen-age mothers who are involved with drugs and inadequate prenatal and nutritional care. Reports of child abuse and neglect from nearby schools, such as P.S. #6 and I.S. #167, reveal a disturbing propensity of neglect and physical abuse of young children.

It should be noted that there is no agency in C.D. #6 which provides service for children who are abused and neglected. Thus the need for this service is paramount within the community.

II.   The Objectives: The purpose of TIP's Family Care Project is to identify families at risk and provide them with appropriate preventive services that will foster stability, prevent institutionalization of children, or in cases where children are institutionalized, hasten their return to the home and community. The goal of TIP's Family Care Project is to provide concrete services to families identified so as to alleviate conditions that create conflict resulting in institutionalization of children and provide to those families whose children have been returned home supports that will prevent a reoccurrence of conditions that precipitated institutionalization in the first place.

TIP's objective is to demonstrate quantitatively and qualitatively that the incidences of abuse, neglect, and recidivism of institutionalized children can be effectively minimized.

III.   Methodology/Approach: TIP's approach was to utilize the Family Care Project Team with the Executive Director being responsible for creating a visible presence in the community through active participation in tenant, block, PTA and Community Planning Board Associations. The staff/team interfaced with the Community Relations Officers of the 48th precinct and emergency personnel of St. Barnabas and Montefiore Hospitals. In short, TIP utilized a wide variety of services provided by more than 56 human service agencies in Community Planning Board #6. At the core of the activities was the goal of creating a level of awareness of services and identification of other key agency personnel who can help families at risk to be more self-reliant and motivated to improve the quality of their own lives.

Trained social workers under the guidance of the Director of Family Services conducted an assessment of families using standard intake procedures and developed plans for concrete services bearing in mind the cultural and behavioral patterns of those families. The social workers were responsible for maintaining records, treatment notes and summaries. They coordinated meetings with family members and related agencies, provided structure, did follow-ups and held all parties accountable to agreed upon goals and objectives. Their specific duties included as follows: individual, family and group counseling, crisis intervention, parenting educational workshops, advocacy, home visits and collaborative efforts with other agencies.

IV.   Results: The Family Care Project of Tremont Improvement Program Neighborhood House was designed to serve families at risk and many of those six hundred (600) families identified by zip codes who have children in foster care. Residents of Community Planning Board #6 and in particular the East Tremont/West Farms communities were to receive individual, group and family counseling in addition to other concrete services as day care, home management, therapy, case work, recreation and remedial skills development. By using interdisciplinary teams of trained social workers and para-professionals, short and long term plans would be mutually developed for families at risk and for youths who were readjusting to the home environment. The planning implementation process was aimed at reducing conflicts which lead to institutionalization of children and develop supports for hastening the return of those in care and maintaining them in their own communities.

Originally we had planned to impact on 75 units for the fiscal year October 1981-September 1982. However, because of the need, we impacted on 118 family units. Of this population, we derived the following breakdown.

1) Prevention entailed 25% of our caseload.
2) Protective entailed 30% of our caseload.
3) Advocacy and referrals consisted of 45% of our caseload.

This reveals that most of our cases entailed advocacy which indicates a need for concrete services; i.e. helping people with public assistance, housing, food stamps, etc. It should be noted that a number of families which were served were in the category of a multiproblem nature.

The ethnic breakdown was as follows according to family units:

Numbers		Percentages
60	Black Families	50.8%
46	Hispanic/Puerto Rican	39.0%
7	Caucasian	6.0%
1	Native American	.8%
2	Mixed (Bl/Wh) Parents have diff. racial background or Asian, N.A.	1.7%
2	Hispanic Non-P.R.	1.7%

A further breakdown of the family units reveals that we actually served 181 clients - men, women and children. This entails the following ethnic breakdown.

Black	Hisp./P.R.	Cauc.	Native Amer.	Asiatic	Hisp. Non-P.R.
104	64	10	1	1	1
57.55%	35.3%	5.5%	.55%	.55%	.55%

This indicates that most of our clients were Black and Hispanic of Puerto Rican descent. They made up 92.85% of our total population served.

In looking at other statistics such as age grouping and sex, we obtain some interesting findings:

Age Group	Persons	%
Under 6	0	0
6 - 17	53	29%
18 - 24	20	11%
25 - 40	59	32.5%
41 - 59	30	16.5%
60 - 64	3	2.0%

65 - older		16	9.0%
	Total	181	100.0%

Sex		Persons	Percentage
Male		72	40%
Female		109	60%
	Total	181	100%

These findings indicate that we have essentially served a young population and that most of our clients, who are from ethnic minority groups, are female.

These findings reflect our needs assessment which was completed prior to the fiscal year of 1981 through 1982. We indicated in that study that "the population of Community District #6 is primarily young, especially between the cohorts of 5-12 through 25-44 years of age."[3]

Of those families which remained with us in treatment, only four (4) families had to place children into residential programs. Of these families, we are describing only 4 children between the ages of 6 through 17 who were placed. This means that we were able to maintain 49 children from 6 through 17 with their families. The percentage of success is quite high - 92% if we base it on the criteria of keeping families together.

Limitations of Demonstration

There were several limitations to this demonstration. One because of cash flow problems, we were unable to hire a clinical staff consisting of a psychiatrist and psychologist and two full-time caseworkers. This prevented us from developing a goal attainment scale to refine and crystallize our effectiveness and our multidisciplinary team was limited in size. Secondly, because we could not hire a full complement of staff, we were limited in counseling a relatively small number of clients. Indeed many of our clients had to be referred to other agencies which had the staffing to help them. Thirdly, it was very difficult to identify families recorded on the CWIS print out in that we had no contract with SSC of New York City. Without a contract, they refused to give us this information. Fourthly, we are hoping to move from our present facilities which are not suitable for counseling services. Current facilities are overcrowded and can affect client's need for confidentiality.

In reference to the above, efforts have been made to obtain private funds to supplement funds. In some instances, we have been successful. We have worked with a psychologist on a volunteer basis. He has offered us a few hours each week. We are also attempting to establish a contract with SSC and are looking for more suitable facilities. Thus every effort has been made to rectify or ameliorate our limitations in this program.

Recommendation:

While staffing has been limited and working conditions and staffing can be improved, our service was comprehensive and we reached a sizable population. It underscores the need for a preventive program in CD #6. Efforts must continue to improve this program and perhaps the emphasis should be to focus on community education and self-help groups rather than on counseling and advocacy.

It should be pointed out that our needs assessment indicates, among other things, that within CD #6 is a high rate of teenage pregnancies.[4] This specifically is the case with the group below the age of 18. With a young population, these are the types of problems generated when services are not available. This need can be addressed by expanding our present teen pregnancy program that focuses on the education of teenagers concerning family planning and includes the support of services that are similar to a family planning program. This program should filter its services to high schools in the area and strong public relations efforts are essential. Instrumental to the success of this program should be interorganizational linkages with social-health agencies. With limited resources for community services, organizational linkages are critical to the survival of agencies and the community. An evaluation mechanism should be incorporated in this program to demonstrate its impact in the community and modifications to improve the service.

Negativism is a likely response to no services to address the high teenage pregnancy crisis. Several spin-off effects can be a catalyst to social health problems. For example, with young parents with limited exposure or experience in rearing children, there is a strong possibility of having a high degree of child abuse and socially dysfunctional children. Children who experience this type of treatment develop into abusive parents themselves. Also, if these young parents are not trained, they are invariably candidates for welfare assistance and possible involvement in crime. Spin-off effects of teenage pregnancy cannot only destroy the quality of life of a community, but also destroy the life of a child. Thus teenage pregnancy services should be given priority by the Family Care Project.

Alternative education and training programs are serious issues to contend with due to its relationship to prepare people with marketable skills for the public and private sector. There is significant consideration for the high school students' reading and mathematical ability. The reading and mathematical scores for the high school population are very low and remedial programs should be examined to address the service population with related support services, such as eye examinations and tutorial services for poor readers.

Another issue for recommendation for the forthcoming year addresses itself to the large numbers of families which are under the aegis of the Child Welfare Foster Care System. According to our data, as of October 31, 1980, there were 2,671 families who were admitted into the system and who reside in the Bronx. Among those families, 614 families or 23.6% of the total number who were admitted, resides in CD #6.[5] This is a rather large percentage and indicated the need for a comprehensive preventive program to prevent placement of youngsters prior to first admission and subsequent to discharge from residential facilities. Indications are that socioeconomic conditions which reveal poverty, housing shortages, high crime, poor sanitation and so forth lead to familial dysfunction and scapegoating which brings about severe acting out and necessitates removal of youngsters from the community. Thus a major focus should be to continue to help children and youth and their families cope more effectively and successfully with stressful social-economic conditions.

MATERIAL REQUEST FORM

I, _____, am requesting that medical
and/or psychiatric material be sent to _____
_____ of TIP-Neighborhood House Inc., Counseling
Services concerning my son/daughter _____ who
was treated from _____

_____
Signature of Parent

_____
TIP COUNSELING SERVICES

TIP FAMILY COUNSELING SERVICES
TIP NEIGHBORHOOD HOUSE INC.,
1028 East 179th Street
Bronx, New York NY 10460

INTAKE SUMMARY FORM

NAME OF CLIENT(S) _____
DATE _____
ADDRESS _____
WORKER _____
TELEPHONE# _____
REFERRAL SOURCE _____

I. PRESENTING PROBLEM

II. CURRENT FUNCTIONING

III. APPROACH TO UTILIZE

IV. GOALS TO ATTAIN

V. PSYCHO SOCIAL EVALUATION

VI. PROGNOSIS

TIP FAMILY COUNSELING SERVICES
of
TIP NEIGHBORHOOD HOUSE, INC.
1028 East 179th Street
Bronx, New York, NY 10460

TRANSFER/DISCHARGE SUMMARY FORM

Name of Client(s) _____

Date _____

ADDRESS _____

Worker _____

Telephone # _____

REFERRAL SOURCE _____

I. PRESENTING PROBLEM

II. THERAPUTIC APPROACH

III. CURRENT FUNCTIONING

IV. GOAL ACHIEVED

V. REASON FOR DISCHARGE

January 7, 1982

Hon. Gertrude Bacon
Parents Anonymous
250 West 57th Street
New York, New York 10107

Dear Judge Bacon:

The following is in reference to our telephone conversation on Thursday, January 14 concerning the facilitation of a Parents Anonymous self help group in community District 6 of the South Bronx. We have set up an initial meeting for parents of this and adjacent communities at the Immanuel Church which is located at 990 East 181 Street in the Bronx. The telephone number is 933-4535.

We would be very pleased if you can attend this meeting and present information about Parents Anonymous to this group.

By car, you can take the West Side Highway, get on the Cross Bronx Expressway and get off at Rosedale Avenue, go around circle and go to East Tremont Avenue. Make a right turn on East Tremont and Southern Blvd. and make a left turn at 181 Street and Southern Blvd. The church should not be far from there.

We look forward to seeing you and we wish you a healthy and Happy New Year.

Sincerely yours,

Allan Mohl, Ph.D., ACSW
Director of Family
and Youth Services (TIP)

3 June 1982

Dear Associate:

TIP was established in 1972 by Phipps Houses, a major non-profit sponsor of low-income housing in the area, to help break the vicious cycle of poverty. By 1975 TIP had become incorporated, established a board of directors, and became a member of United Neighborhood Houses.

In 1981 the Family Counseling Service of TIP was established.

Family Counseling Services provides a variety of services to the entire Bronx Community.

These services include information and referral, short and long term counseling, family or marriage counseling, group counseling and self-help groups. (As of 6/9/82, TIP now sponsors a Parents Anonymous group).

TIP's priority for the coming year is to address the high incidence of abuse and institutionalization of children - a problem finally beginning to command the local and national attention it deserves. We will be working with families identified as needing preventive services through one-to-one casework, group counseling and linkages with community medical facilities and parenting support groups. This falls in with our entire Family Counseling Services approach, aimed at Keeping Families Together and helping them to receive the services they need.

If there are any questions or a need for further information, please call or contact:

Mr. Allan Mohl, Ph.D. - (212) 893-1224

5 June 1982

Dear Associate:

In 1981 the Family Counseling Services of T.I.P. was established. Our program is the outgrowth of the State Department of Social Services efforts to provide preventive services to the people of the Bronx.

These services include information and referral, short and long term counseling, family or marriage counseling, group counseling and self-help groups. (as of 6/9/82, TIP now sponsors a Parents' Anonymous group).

There are two very important ways you can help us. First, by referring prospective clients to our service. Secondly, by sending us a letter verifying that you will make TIP's services available to prospective clients. We are asking for a verification letter, as it is required by the State Department of Social Services. Thus, you will play an important role in keeping this much needed service for the people of the Bronx community.

If this program proves successful, we hope that it will serve as a model for other similar programs.

For further information, please contact myself, Allan Mohl, Ph.D. at (212) 893-1224.

TIP looks forward to continuing working with you, thanks for your cooperation and effort.

Sincerely,

Allan Mohl, Ph.D., ACSW
Project Director

17 June 1982

Classified
Bronx Press Review
1924 Cross Bronx Expressway
Bronx, New York 10472

Dear Sirs:

I wish Co have a small display for a Parents' Anonymous self-help group which meets at TIP Neighborhood House each Wednesday at 5:15 P.M. until 7:00 P.M.

The display should read as follows:

"Parents!.. Are your children getting on your nerves? Are the day to day hardships of living getting you down?.... There is help in a confidential and private setting. No names mentioned! No agency affiliation needed! No Fees! If interested, please call - Monday thru Friday; 9 AM - 5 P.M. 893-1224. Ask for Adrienne or Allan.

I am enclosing a check for $ 11.34.

A small news item will be forthcoming.

Sincerely,

Allan Mohl, Ph.D., CSW
TIP Neighborhood House

August 2, 1982

Mr. Allan Mohl, Ph.D., ACSW
Project Director
Family Counseling Services, T.I.P.
Neighborhood House, Inc.
1028 East 179th Street
Bronx, N.Y. 10460

Dear Mr. Mohl:

The Adolescent Pregnancy Care and Prevention Program of The Southwest Bronx Youth Services Project, Inc. willingly supports the Family Counseling Services of T.I.P. as a program which is both viable and necessary for families of the Bronx.

We look forward to working with the staff of the program and to referring the young people we come in contact with to the various components of the program.

We wish you much success in your new endeavor.

Sincerely,

Denise Shepard
Deputy Director

DS/am

NEW YORK FOUNDLING HOSPITAL
BRONX TEEN PARENTING PROGRAM
384 East 149th Street - 5th Floor
Bronx, New York 10455
212-292-9057

August 3, 1982

Mr. Allan Mohl, Ph.D., ACSW
Project Director
Family Counseling Services of T.I.P.
1028 E. 178th. Street
Bronx, N.Y. 10460

Dear Mr. Mohl,

I am in receipt of your recent letter, and very pleased to learn of another preventive program in the Bronx.

Reviewing the services you offer, I am certain some of our clients and more specifically referrals that we can't accept; would be able to benefit from your program. Information on your program will be shared with these clients, and every effort will be made to encourage them to take advantage of it.

Kindly let me know if there are any specific criteria for referrals, and if there is any additional way in which Bronx Teen Parenting can be of help to you.

Sincerely,

Mrs. Robyn Brown Manning, CSW
Project Coordinator
Bronx Teen Parenting Program

CHAPTER VI

Sexual Abuse of the Child: A Treatment Model for the Incestuous Family

Abstract: From September '79 through July '80, I was the supervisor of the Incest Treatment Unit at Queensboro Society for the Prevention of Cruelty to Children. During this period, I was instrumental in implementing a family treatment unit for incestuous families which was unique within the metropolitan area of New York City.

The paper which follows was presented by me at a meeting of the Teen Outreach Pregnancy Prevention Program under the aegis of the New York City Board of Education and the 2nd Annual Conference of the Bronx Child Abuse and Neglect Task Force whose title was Helping Hands For Abused Children. This paper evolved from my work as a supervisor for the above-mentioned Incest Treatment Unit. It specifies that a family approach to child abuse is the best method of treatment. The paper states that concurrent psychotherapy for the child, each parent, the marital dyad and family treatment was part of the treatment program. Ancillary treatment included group therapy. In addition, family members were encouraged to participate in self-help groups. Frequently, the threat of criminal prosecution was necessary to maintain perpetrators - usually fathers or boyfriends - in treatment.

Introduction: Sexual abuse of pre-adolescent children is being reported with alarming frequency. This increase is a result of professionals' growing awareness of the incidence of sexual abuse, more open communication regarding sexuality, the availability of communication services for abused children, and reporting techniques that are more protective of sexually abused children.

Studies indicate that children are often the victims of sexual assault and abuse by persons known to them. The dynamics of affected families have been explored, and Vincent DeFrances in his article, Protecting the Child Victim of Sex Crimes Committed by Adults (Denver, Colo.; American Humane Association, 1969) suggests that a large percentage of such families were multi-problem with the father suffering from hostile, aggressive behavior. He concluded that approximately two-thirds of the victims developed emotional disturbances as a result of the sexual abuse.[1] Renee Brant and Veronica Tisza in an article, The Sexually Misused Child, which appeared in the American Journal of Orthopsychiatry, 47 (January 1977) suggest factors in the family's constellation that may increase a child's risk of sexual abuse, including a parent who was sexually abused as a child or a parent who is single.[2] It is clear that physicians and social workers in the field of mental health must respond to sexually abused children and provide the necessary services for their protection.

Jerilyn A. Shamroy, a medical social worker, describes a study done at her facility, Children's Hospital Medical Center in Cincinnati, Ohio in an article, A Perspective on Childhood Sexual Abuse, which appeared in Social Work, Vol. 25, No. 2, March '80 issue, pp. 128-131.

"From January 1977 through December 1977, seventy-eight children were treated at Children's Hospital for sexual abuse based on medical evidence, venereal disease, or the child's account of molestation. Their ages ranged from 1 year, 11 months to 12 years, 7 months. Sixty-four were females, and fourteen were males. Children from 1 to 5 years of age constituted 47 percent of the total. Twenty-four of the 78 children were admitted to Children's Hospital for injuries, venereal disease or because of the family's inability to protect the child adequately ... Sexual abuse must always be considered when a child is seen with venereal disease, vaginal discharge or genital irritation".[3]

Children abused by persons known to them, including a natural father or stepfather, experienced a high degree of anxiety and ambivalence. If the abuser subsequently was excluded from the family, the child's guilt and ambivalence increased, particularly if court action was involved and testimony from the child was needed. Many of these children had experienced affection from the abuser and wanted the family to reunite. When the abuser was an extended family member or neighbor, the child was often criticized or ostracized because family loyalties were divided. The most common reaction of the victim's mother was avoidance and/or denial. She wished to forget that the incident had occurred and believed that follow-up counseling would make it more difficult for herself and her child. All the victimized children and their families were offered counseling to help them express and work through their feelings. The majority of families did not follow through, however. The families most willing to accept follow-up therapy were the ones faced with impending court action.

I believe that a family approach to child abuse is the best method of treatment. Even if the abuser is a stranger, the entire family will be affected by the incident and family life will be altered. Often the reaction of adults disturbs the child more than the sexual activity. Some children seem to react with apparent indifference or to relish the attention of the abuser until they observe the shock and anger of the adults around them. Community agencies such as family and child guidance clinics, rape crisis centers and mental health clinics are valuable resources, although many have long waiting lists.

The Incest Treatment Unit of QSPCC (My own experience)

I think it is very important to mention one's orientation in talking about child sexual abuse. Although it cannot be proved as yet, I believe that there are different populations of child sexual abuse. The population which appears initially in an emergency room may be qualitatively different from the population which first comes to a VD clinic. These populations may very well differ from those which initially commit the statutory child protection agency or the police. There may well be still other differences in the population of child sexual abuse cases which initially contact a child guidance clinic or a mental health agency or a mental health practitioner in private practice. I make these presumptions because I think that our experiences which are very child-protection oriented, are substantially different from those acquired in programs that are more offender-oriented (for example, the Child Sexual Abuse Treatment Program of the Santa Clara County, Department of Probation) or more crisis intervention-oriented (for example, the Harborview Sexual Assault Center in Seattle) or a combination of child protective and family oriented as we were at Q.S.P.C.C.

At QSPCC, we worked closely with the Queens Family Court. The protective worker usually handled the court details and the ongoing therapy was done by the Incest Treatment worker. If the perpetrator who was usually separated from the family subsequent to the initial court hearing, repeated sexual abusive behavior, he would be returned to court by the assigned protective worker. The thrust however, was to work ultimately with the entire family and help the perpetrator go back to the family constellation. Our feeling was that the victim should remain in the home and not, as too often occurs, be placed in a foster care facility, or with a relative outside of the home. It was felt that to do so increases the victim's sense of guilt.

It is important to recognize that there are laws against child sexual abuse and/or incest in all 50 states. According to New York State Penal Law, incest is a felony defined as an act of marrying or engaging in "sexual intercourse with a person whom he knows to be related to him either legitimately or illegitimately as an ancestor, descendant, brother or sister or either the whole or the half blood, uncle, aunt, nephew or niece." Sexual abuse, a misdemeanor, relates to sexual contact such as touching the genitals.

Most of the families we worked with in the ITU at QSPCC were families in which fondling of the genitals was the presenting problem. While the state penal law's definition of incest is intercourse, such a definition excludes a good deal of the reported sexual activity with younger children because intercourse is not usually attempted with latency aged females. Many long-term, emotionally charged intra-family sexual relations do not involve intercourse, but appear to be quite similar in intensity and duration to ones that do. Therefore, researchers and those of us in the helping professions have usually included in their definition of incest such obviously sexual acts as oral-genital contact, fondling of breast and genitals and/or buttocks, and mutual masturbation. At QSPCC, one of the criteria for referral into the Incest Treatment Unit was specified as follows: "The Unit will treat incestuous families in which fondling, oral-genital sex and/ or sexual intercourse or any sexual exploitation by a family member has occurred."[4]

The Dynamics of Child Sexual Assault

Let's talk about the dynamics of child sexual assault or abuse. I believe we are not talking about a capricious, unpredictable, unplanned phenomenon. Instead, I think for the most part, the perpetrator is someone who has access to the child. The perpetrator must also be someone who has the opportunity to establish a sexual relationship with a child. Opportunity can almost be equated with privacy in these cases. The phenomenon usually takes place with the perpetrator and the child being alone with each other -- rarely when anyone else is around or as part of a group phenomenon. Who, then, is the perpetrator likely to be? Almost always someone in the child's own family -- someone who has access and opportunity within the family circle. Or the perpetrator may be someone given access to the child by the parents or guardian - again someone within the child's daily sphere of activities. Where do we allow little children to be? And with whom? We let them be at home, we let them go to school, we let them engage in age-appropriate organized group activity such as church groups, boy scouts, girl scouts, clubs and so forth. People who are likely to have access to the child are likely to be known to the child in one of these spheres. Thus the dynamics of child sexual abuse usually involves a known adult who is in a legitimate power position over a child and who exploits the usual accepted patterns of dominance and authority that our society permits adults to have over children. The exploitation and misuse of accepted power relationships is a highly significant aspect of the dynamics of child sexual abuse.

Now how does the perpetrator engage the child? How does the perpetrator get the child to participate in some kind of a sexual relationship? Usually he or she does so by approaching the child in a non-threatening way, depending on the age of the child - possibly by presenting the activity as a game. There is usually a verbal or non-verbal misrepresentation of moral standards on the part of the adult. In other words, the adult conveys to the child "this is ok" and the child accepts this because in our society, children usually look toward adults to provide guidelines for what is right and acceptable behavior. There may be rewards offered for the participation. So the child becomes engaged in sexual activity usually without force, without violence, without injury and frequently, if the perpetrator is adept, without threat and without fear.[5]

As mentioned before, sexual abuse runs the gamut of sexual behavior from mutual masturbation to sexual intercourse. In the incestuous family, it is a conditioning process and it begins at an early age for the child and may progress through the years ultimately to sexual intercourse.

The Secrecy Phase

What do all these dynamics and mechanics lead to? A child has been engaged in some kind of sexual behavior which is then followed by an extremely important phase of the activity so far as the child is concerned and so far as the future development of the case is concerned -- the secrecy phase. The perpetrator's primary agenda after the sexual behavior is to get the child to keep their activity a secret in that he obviously does not want to get caught; he does not want the child to blow the whistle on their sexual activity. Presumably he would like the activity to continue. And so the child is then usually gently led into a phase in which he/she comes to understand that the special activity between them must be kept secret from others.

The child usually does keep the secret in that rewards have probably been offered. Possibly there may have been threats made - the less adept the perpetrator, the more likely he is to use threats. If threats were used to enforce the secrecy, they should be carefully assessed for the degree of physical violence proposed, if any. Of course many compelling types of threats for a child will not include physical violence. For example, the perpetrator may threaten the child with anger by a third party ("If you tell mommy, she'll be awfully mad at us.") Or the threat may involve separation ("If you tell anybody, Mommy may divorce me or I may go to jail.") The personal separation threat may be used, which is highly anxiety-provoking for a child ("If you tell anyone, you will be sent away.") or the threat may involve self-harm by the perpetrator ("If you tell anybody, I'll kill myself.") Lastly, the threat may involve violence against the child ("If you tell anybody, I'll hurt you or kill you.") In assessing and categorizing these threats, two elements deserve particular attention. First, the degree of physical violence threatened and second, was any part of the threat ever carried out? A good child protection assessment of any sexual abuse case will include a careful look at all these dynamics inherent in the secrecy phase.

There is still another important reason why the child keeps the secret. The sexual behavior, if introduced by a known and valued perpetrator who does not hurt the child, tends to be self reinforcing. In other words, the child keeps the secret because she or he likes it and wants the behavior to continue. We are, after all, talking about pleasant non-violent stimulation - activity that feels good. Although we behave as if children are born without genitals or at least without the cerebral equipment to appreciate genital stimulation, the fact is that a child's sexuality begins at birth. To ignore that, the child may very well find the sexual activity with the perpetrator pleasurable, and that the pleasurable aspects may be a motive for the child to wish to continue the behavior over time is not only to ignore the obvious but to miss some of the most important dynamics.[6]

If we take cognizance of the point that child sexual abuse is a conditioning process and on a continuum over time, we then recognize that the incident which precipitates any investigation has never been the first incident of sexual abuse experienced by a victim. This holds true for both intra-family cases and extra-family cases whenever an adequate investigation has been done.

The Disclosure Phase

Sooner or later we are going to come to another important phase - the disclosure phase. When the child victim, in most reported cases its a female, finds out her friends have sex with peers and not their fathers, she feels guilty and angry and seeks revenge, then she may report the behavior herself. This child is usually an adolescent or a pre-adolescent. This youngster may become interested in dating and staying out late even though an incestuous sexual relationship is continued. Such adolescents may receive increasing pressure to maintain the family fortress and meet all psychological needs within the family circle. When this occurs, the child may tell the secret, not because the primary item on the agenda is to stop the sexual abuse activity but rather in pursuit of some other goal. Those of us who receive complaints of child sexual abuse usually assume that the child complained because he/she is primarily interested in stopping the abuse. Frequently this assumption is incorrect. These children often recant when they see how much family disruption will be caused or they recant because the pressure situation which drove them to make the complaint is altered.

This sexual abuse secret may be disclosed accidentally. Perhaps the perpetrator was not very adept - someone saw the sexual activity and told about it. Or the perpetrator may accidentally hurt the child and the physical trauma brings the case to light. Or the child may get VD, particularly gonorrhea. Or perhaps, if it's a female victim, she becomes pregnant.

Validating the Complaint

Even with competent and thorough evaluation and examination, we can expect to find corroborating physical evidence in a small proportion of cases. How, then, does one validate a complaint of child sexual abuse? For the most part, validation will depend on investigative interviewing, bringing on the assessment skills and previous experience of the interviewer or interviewers. It requires a skilled and knowledgeable interviewer who is willing to believe. One of the basic hurdles for the interviewer to overcome is a mental attitude which holds that children routinely make allegations of sexual abuse by adults, practically as a rite of passage. This mental attitude further holds that children either lie about sexual abuse or fantasize its occurrence or both. The skilled and knowledgeable interviewer is not going to be hampered by such a mental attitude. Instead he or she is prepared to accept the credibility of the detailed and explicit description of sexual activity which can often be elicited from the victim using the specialized interviewing skills which are required. I know of no other clinical situation in which the interviewer's pay-off for denial of the situation equals or exceeds that of the participants. In other words we have so much investment in declaring the complaint invalid that we bend over backwards to throw it out - to turn the case into a non-case by not believing that sexual abuse actually occurred.

According to Dr. Alex Zaphiris of the School of Social Work at Houston University in Texas, psychological testing which utilizes the TAT and Rorsbach tests can reveal whether the alleged victim is an actual incest victim or has made a false allegation.[7] Zaphiris describes what he calls an incestuogenic pattern (actual). The dynamics reveal that the victim has feelings of guilt. She/he will then reverse her/his allegations. The victim will stipulate that he/she lied. The psychological testing (TAT/Rorsbach) will reveal no sexual fantasy or hostility.

In a case of allegation only in which incest does not exist, there is what we call a retaliation fantasy. There is no incestuogenic pattern. The victim does not reverse her claim that incest occurred, reveals no guilt. The testing indicates the presence of sexual fantasy and hostility.

Actual Incest

A)   Incestuogenic Pattern
      dynamics - characteristics
      victim - guilt
B)   Reversal of victim
      (claims she/he lied)
C)   Psychological Test
      TAT/Rorsbach
      Reveals no sexual fantasy or hostility

Allegations

A)   Motive - retaliation fantasy
B)   No incestuogenic pattern
      Victim - has no guilt
C)   No reversal

Psychological Test

There is presence of sexual fantasy and hostility. Indicators based on verbal and psychological exploration are important in determining whether actual incest occurred or allegations occurred. Where there is an absence of sexual fantasy and hostility then the victim has experienced incest in that the victim does not need to have sexual fantasy and is actually experiencing or has experienced the real thing.

What other elements are required for successful intervention with child sexual abuse besides skilled investigative interviewing? Thorough knowledge of the child abuse and sexual assault laws is essential. An ability to engage the sexually abused child and his/her family members is also important. This is just as important in cases involving extra-family perpetrators as in incest cases.

The Engagement Process - The Question of Intervention

The dynamics of child sexual abuse are such that family participants will rarely come to us asking for help and follow through with the consistence that our current philosophy of helping services demands. The incestuous father is usually a "me first person" who very frequently has the entire family revolving around him and meeting his needs. This father encourages all family members to erect a "family fortress." The outside world is perceived as hostile and all family members are pressured to limit contacts with peers and outsiders and instead meet all psychological needs within the family circle. He is usually quite immature, very rigid and extremely likely to react to disclosure with denial.

According to Zaphiris, the father, the usual perpetrator, is not sick, ill, or disturbed. He does not fit any pathological category. The only malfunctioning is that he addresses his sexual activity to his child.[8] However, he does concur and I agree that the incestuous father is frequently selfish, egocentric and narcissistic.

What about the mother? She is usually also immature and is frequently a very dependent person. She has failed to protect the children and may have conscious or unconscious knowledge that the sexual abuse has taken place. Occasionally the mother has set up the child for sexual abuse. Mother is frequently about when the sexual abuse is taking place. She may be very competitive with the target child.

According to Barbara Brooks, a psychologist from New York Hospital-Cornell Medical Center, Westchester Division, in her paper, Familial Influences in Father-Daughter Incest... psychological tests given to mothers in incestuous families present evidence of depression and unconscious homosexual trends. This suggests that these unconscious trends play an important role in the mother's inability to act as a restraining agent, that is, according to Brooks, mother sends father to do what she cannot permit of herself.[9]

The background of mothers in families in which overt father-daughter incest occurs are, like their husbands, characterized by a high degree of rejection and maternal deprivation. Unfortunately, the hostile-dependent mother-daughter relationship is then carried by the mother and blossoms again in her relationship with the daughter who later becomes sexually intimate with the father. Brooks would argue that the projection on to the daughter of the hostility derived from the bad maternal object representation is subsequently identified with by the mother in an attempt to work through her own difficulty with the maternal grandmother and that the mechanism of projective identification plays a pivotal role in facilitating the occurrence of incest.

A number of investigators have emphasized the role-reversal between mothers and daughters in incestuous families. Implied in this role reversal is a special, wife-like relationship with the father. The investigators further note that having succeeded in setting up the daughter as "little mothers", the mother gradually became dependent on her in a child-like fashion and began to displace her hostile feelings for her own mother on to her daughter.

Other investigators of the incestuous family have noted the absence of a consistent maternal object and the role reversal and suggests that for the daughter incest is connected with basic oral dependent needs; although girls in these cases seem to be too much attached to their fathers, it develops that their activities with the father primarily provide satisfaction of revenge wishes against the mother for oral frustrations.

Let's turn now to the other children in the family. They are frequently aware of the special relationship between the target child and the perpetrator. They may have been victims themselves at one point and indeed, may have "set up" the sibling who is currently the victim. They are usually very competitive and may be very angered by the family disruption which ensues at the time of disclosure. These siblings may be very unreceptive to and uncooperative with the interviewer who enters the situation and proposes to "handle" the problem by instituting lots of changes.

What about the target child? Since most reports of incest involve father-daughter, let's look at the female victim. The child victim almost always has the expectation that we are going to perform magic. The child may now be regretting the disclosure and wants us to waive a magic wand and somehow change the situation painlessly, without disruption and, hopefully, without telling the parents that the disclosure has been made.

Opinion is divided as to whether incest leads to pervasive psychopathology in the daughter. One group tends to argue that the experience of a child in a sex relationship with an adult does not always seem to have traumatic effects. That is, in many cases, the experience offers an opportunity to test out in reality an infantile fantasy, the consequences of which are found to be not only less severe than anticipated, but gratifying and pleasurable.

Recently, what might be called a "pro-incest" lobby has merged. Led by sex researchers, the pro-incest literature suggests that incest between children and adults can be beneficial and that opposition to incest reflects an "uptight" society.[10]

On the other hand, there is no lack of reports of traumatic outcomes of such sexual experiences. Contrary to the pro-incest lobby, there appears to be a significant association between the report of incest and serious psychopathology. For child victims, there are higher incidences of somatic complaints, sexual precociousness, confusion, depression, and subsequently a sense of shame and guilt. These emotions are shown to endure for a long term. Main trends which show up on psychological testing done shortly after the detection of the incest are depression, anxiety, confused sexual identity, fear of sexuality, oral deprivation and oral sadism. Defensive operations include denial, repression and projection. Moreover, it is noted that cognitive functioning is often lower than potential. Clinicians suggest that efforts to blot out traumatic memories have spread into a generalized fear of retention of any type of knowledge; for example, it has been suggested that one indication of an ongoing incest is a precipitous drop in school performance.

Treatment - Possibilities for Success

As former supervisor of the ITU at QSPCC, we utilized concepts of philosophy in treating the incestuous family based on a synthesis of Alex Zaphiris who maintained that one's focus is only on incest and on Hank Giarretto who believes in a humanistic psychology. Both agree that the therapist must do individual, marital, dyadic, family and group counseling. At QSPCC, we maintained, and this concept was based essentially on Giarretto's approach, that during early phases of treatment, family members required a deeper commitment than the one usually expected from a counselor. The families which were treated at the ITU at QSPCC were invariably burdened with various pressing problems such as housing, financial, and legal needs. Consequently, the therapist found himself/herself acting as liaison between the family and the community resources that could meet these practical needs.

Giarretto, while developing a Child Sexual Abuse Treatment Program at San Jose, California, recognized that incestuous families are badly fragmented as a result of the original dysfunctional family dynamics which are further exacerbated upon disclosure to civil authorities. He concluded that the child, mother and father must be treated separately before family counseling becomes productive.[11] Consequently, the treatment procedure is normally applied in this order:

1) Individual counseling, particularly for the child and mother and later for the father.
2) Mother-daughter counseling.
3) Marital counseling which becomes a key treatment if the family wishes to be reunited.
4) Father-daughter counseling.
5) Family counseling.
6) Group counseling.

The treatments are neither listed in order of importance nor followed invariably in each case, but usually all are required for family reconstitution. The typical strategy is to reconcile the daughter-mother relationship and to rebuild the family around this dyad.

At QSPCC, a combined authoritative and supportive approach seemed most effective to the child sexual abuse cases we encountered. The authoritative handle, in our experience, must be that of court involvement. Lesser incentives have not been effective in maintaining the family in treatment or, indeed, in maintaining access to the target child.

Maintaining access to the child is a critical feature in these cases, and again, requires the authoritative "handle". The child and all "cooperative" individuals are nearly always under enormous pressure from other family members - especially the perpetrator - to recant and move away from a cooperative stance and involvement in treatment. Our insistence in maintaining access to the child and encouragement to family members to form relationships with therapists and peers in group therapy is a critical factor in breaking down the incestuous family fortress.

Role modeling is an important aspect of treatment for all family members. Opportunities for role modeling abound in both individual and group therapy. The use of multiple therapists and co-therapists in group and couples therapy provide further opportunity to use this technique on many levels.

We recognize that innovative treatment programs have been developed for the treatment of whole families in which incest has been detected. At the ITU, frequently by court order, the father was separated from the family but allowed to maintain visiting rights. The family was stipulated by the judge to continue treatment. The goal of therapy may be or may not be to get the parents back together again.

Concurrent psychotherapy for the child, each parent, the marital dyad and family treatment was part of the treatment program. Ancillary included group therapy. In addition, family members were encouraged to participate in self-help groups. Frequently, the threat of criminal prosecution was necessary to maintain fathers in treatment.

The goals of family treatment at the ITU were:

1) To intervene effectively in the family so as to prevent a recurrence of incest with the identified child or any other sibling.
2) To foster a familial environment in which a) the marital system is emotionally gratifying; b) children have appropriate roles sexually and are allowed to separate and individuate; c) all members of the family are able to regain a sense of control and power over their own lives.

In Conclusion

I am convinced that there is no single professional discipline that knows all the answers to this problem. There is no single professional discipline which prepares one to be an "expert" or a "therapist" or an "investigator" in child sexual abuse. Lastly, there is no single professional discipline that owns child sexual abuse in that territorial way that we divide up and fight over most of the other problems which interest us. Actually, there has been relatively little effort to divide up child sexual abuse. For the most part, it has been nobody's child -- possibly because most people are so perplexed about how to approach the problem or deal with it. Willingness to push into unchartered territories, to join hands with individuals from other disciplines to work toward a common goal, to experience frustration and pain and make mistakes -- all are required. Finally, a commitment to stick with these cases and programs long enough to learn or relearn skills in working with resistant and/or involuntary clients is essential. I am deliberately drawing a grim yet realistic picture. The excitement and occasional reward of learning new skills and helping troubled people take even small steps toward a healthier lifestyle cannot be conveyed -- you have to experience them for yourselves.

CHAPTER VII

New Approaches in Treating a Population Change in a Temporary Care Facility

Abstract: As Director of Residential Social Services at Queensboro Society for the Prevention of Cruelty to Children from September '77 through August '79, I was part of an administrative staff which developed and implemented a unit system in a short-term facility for emotionally disturbed adolescents. The following paper describes the system which enabled a variety of disturbed youngsters to function satisfactorily in a rather crowded environment. I attempt to point out, within this paper, that a general assessment indicated that the physical plant, while not adequate, was not primary in the behavioral improvement of the residents. Essentially it is the interaction of staff and children and the system's set-up to support the interaction which is primary to effectuating change.

Introduction: The Queensboro Society for the Prevention of Cruelty to Children was founded in 1929 when this Agency opened a non-sectarian shelter to house 45 neglected, dependent, abused and destitute children. Over the years, the role of the Society has expanded so that now the Agency provides comprehensive service to children and their families. In addition to the Diagnostic Residence, which currently houses approximately 50 youngsters,[1] QSPCC operates two long-term group homes for 12 children each[2] that, under the auspices of the Agency is a protective services division to investigate and intervene in abuse and maltreatment of children; and a preventive services program whose services include the direct attempt to prevent foster placement.

In the last two years, the population of the temporary care residence has changed dramatically. In the past, the youngster coming into care had been neglected by his parents or was temporarily placed due to an emergency or crisis such as illness of a parent. At that time, the population of the Residence was mixed in terms of an age grouping between 8 and 18 years and was fairly equally divided between boys and girls. Although these youngsters were often experiencing a great deal of anxiety and stress, staff was able to deal with these problems through providing a good deal of attention and support. A major positive factor was that frequently parents or guardians were still involved and, with counseling and guidance, the family could be reunited. Even when long-term care or placement with a relative was the final plan, these youths had the knowledge that their parents were still involved in the planning. The experience that all levels of staff had developed in the many years of dealing with a similar population was a crucial factor in helping the youngsters to maximize and aid in long-term planning.

Recently the population of children coming into the Diagnostic Residence has changed from one that was an age mixture of youngsters to a population of male and female adolescents who are acting-out and frequently emotionally troubled and disturbed. Now over (3/4) three-quarters of the youngsters in the QSPCC Residence are court referred as Persons in Need of Supervision (PINS). Often the PINS petition is taken out by a parent who can no longer handle the child because of acting out behavior or, as frequent in the case of girls, sexual promiscuity. Sometimes the PINS is taken out by an Agency when a child acts out, runs away or cannot get along in a foster home. Because of the change in youngsters in care, QSPCC has seen the need to provide specialized treatment services for the disturbed adolescent.

The change of age and type of youngster coming into placement is confirmed by an analysis done by the program planning division of New York City's Special Services for Children which is the public agency that has the overall responsibility in the city for monitoring the more than ninety private agencies which operate foster care and child welfare facilities. The analysis found that there was a projected deficit of 1,100 spaces for older and handicapped children resulting in the need for the development of programs for adolescents with special needs.[3]

The need for some children to be placed in a facility, such as our Diagnostic Reception Center or Intake Unit has been discussed in the literature, particularly with reference to the provision of temporary care until a plan is established for long-range goals. For example, Alan Keith-Lucas and Clifford W. Sanford have discussed the benefits of a good child care facility. They have indicated that among the merits of this type of facility are "eliminating conflicts between two sets of parenting figures; it is particularly helpful for the child who can profit from group interaction, for the child who has difficulty trusting adults, and the child in need of socialization."[4]

Many of the characteristics discussed above are exhibited by our current residential population. One major problem noted was a high number of youngsters in our Residence going AWOL (running away). This was something which had become a pattern of behavior for many of the adolescents prior to coming to the Diagnostic Residence. Many of the youngsters whom we admitted had been chronic runaways from home or had had this problem in foster homes or other child care facilities. A large number of these youngsters had, prior to placement in the Residence, been in a number of other agencies and had failed to be able to succeed or fit into their programs due to acting out behavior, running away, and/or problems in forming relationships. These youngsters were frequently hostile to authority figures and engaged in fighting among their peers. Another major problem which was exhibited by many of our teenagers was sexual acting out. Almost all of the boys and girls had experimented with sex on a frequent basis. Approximately 5% of the girls who had resided at our Residence had abortions and another 5% had babies either before or after entering into our program.

Currently there are two girls living in our Diagnostic Residence who have babies. Despite the high rate of sexual experience, these youngsters are often ignorant concerning their own biological make-up and the linkage between sex and love and the responsibilities toward another person. The basic facts about birth control are often lacking. Indeed, occasionally there are youngsters who do not know the relationship between sexual intercourse and pregnancy.

It was obvious to staff that a different set of techniques was necessary to treat the child now coming into care who had different problems than those who were admitted in the past. It was the general feeling that a plan had to be worked out to deal with the acting out and self-destructive behavior of these youths and to break the pattern of failure that accompanied this. Thus, it was decided by unit heads, after discussion and input from line child care and social work staff, to implement the following approaches:

1) A change in structure to a unit system with a complete diagnostic plan for each child.
2) Behavior modification.

Behavior Modification

The behavior modification system that was developed involved a point system which was designed to reinforce positive behavior and discourage negative behavior. The emphasis was on encouraging good behavior and acts toward peers and others.

Charles Schaefer has indicated twenty-five guidelines to assist child care counselors in disciplining children in residential care. These guidelines include: (1) being explicit about linking misbehavior with the penalty, (2) developing a supportive relationship, (3) and avoiding inconsistencies.[5] In determining the points to be allotted to each youngster, the concepts by Schaefer were emphasized so that the youth clearly understood the relationships between gaining or losing points on his or her behavior. For example, each adolescent was expected to attend school and was rewarded 175 points for perfect attendance for a week. The points were accrued on a 24 hour basis each day. Points were accrued for both effort made and for performance. For example, a youngster would accumulate points if he or she went to school and would receive additional points if he or she tried in school and stayed out of trouble. Points would be lost if the youngster fought in class, cursed the teachers and, in general, acted in an obnoxious and destructive manner. If enough points were lost, the child could drop to level 2. Certain privileges would be withdrawn as a result. The lowest level to which a child could drop was level 3. At this level a youngster had no privileges. He or she did not receive an allowance or was given a weekend pass. In some instances, the child was not to participate in certain activities such as trips or shows.

This level system which is interrelated to the accrual of points for youngsters has an enormous impact on the behavior of children if the system is implemented in a consistent manner. All staff were oriented to the point system and social workers, child care counselors, teachers and other staff were to see to it that the points were being given out and/or taken away appropriately. Points were also earned for respect of property, good peer relations, attending rap sessions with the social workers and other group meetings. On the other hand, points were lost for using bad language, failure to attend school, disrespect for peers or staff. Severe penalties were given for going "AWOL" or using alcohol, reefers or other drugs. As shown on chart I, earning the maximum (1500) number of points meant that the youngster was on Level I (1500 points) and was entitled to the privileges of a $5.00 allowance per week, an afternoon pass, and other privileges. A youngster on Level II had earned 1000 points and was entitled to $2.50 allowance and an afternoon pass. A youngster on Level III received $1.00 or no allowance and minimal to no privileges. Severe penalties - no level - could consist of a loss of allowance, no pass, room restriction or work detail. An individual placed on work detail could not earn any additional points until the task was completed. The work was related to the youth's negative behavior, i.e. writing graffiti on the wall would consist of having to clean up the entire wall as an assignment. Target behavior, or specific areas which needed strengthening, were determined by social workers and/or child care workers in conjunction with the resident. Points could be added or subtracted by working on these areas. Prior to the implementation of the point system, youngsters had been frequently acting out; vandalism, stealing, absconding from the residential area, fighting among peers and general mayhem was the norm.

However, with the implementation of the point system, there was a considerable reduction on the above-mentioned behavioral patterns. For example, reduction in running away was most dramatic. Where at one point it was averaging 20% of the population, it was reduced to less than 1% of the population. These factors alone reveal that the point system, when implemented properly and consistently, brought about dramatic results.

It should be noted, too, that all new admissions to the program were told about the point system in detail by their caseworkers and the child care staff who supervised them. This helped to bring about a positive anticipation within many of the youngsters who were admitted. With the aid of the point system, children were more amenable to casework.

Youngsters such as Annette G., a 14 year old girl who was diagnosed as retarded and who set up a scapegoat role for herself, began to feel safer and more secure and was, therefore, more amenable to her caseworker. Annette began to believe and relate more appropriately in time to others and her scapegoat status among her peers was eventually mitigated.

Another youngster, David P., a 13 year old, who was diagnosed as schizophrenic and who was viewed as limited, initially refused to take off his clothes at night, slept with his head on the bed and his feet on the floor. In time, as he began to feel more secure, he was able to sleep in bed in pajamas, and his overall behavior indicated real progress toward developing good peer relations.

These two youngsters typify some of the gains made by youngsters within a unit system in which both a behavioral modification approach and more traditional approaches were utilized to effectuate some behavioral pattern changes or modifications. Both traditional casework methods and a point system or behavioral modification approach were implemented in such a way that both fed into each other and became interdependent on each other as part of a total therapeutic milieu.

A similar type of reward system was proven successful in Cunningham Children's Home in Urbana, Illinois where an incentive program was utilized to attempt to change youngsters' negative acts into responsible behavior.[6] Similar to the program at Q.S.P.C.C., each child was placed at a level according to behavior and this was tied to allowances and other privileges. As compared with Q.S.P.C.C., the program was easy to begin because of staff support.[7] The success of this program and others of its type was encouraging to staff and served as a model for the development of the Q.S.P.C.C. Point System. It was the thinking of staff that if a system of this kind could work in similar institutions, then it had a good chance of success at Q.S.P.C.C., all things being equal.

The Unit System

Reorganizing became a high priority to deal with the 80% of the residential population who had been in the foster care system at least five years, were academically functioning at a minimum of three grades below level, and were angry and scared. Another priority was to maintain a low staff "burnout" rate. The reorganization evolved out of a thorough assessment of the general characteristics of the client population and the difficulty in finding appropriate placement quickly for challenging adolescents. During the process of a complete evaluation and diagnostic work-up, a youngster was assigned to either Unit A or Unit B. An assignment to Unit A was the recognition that securing placement for a particular child would be difficult.[8] The difficulties may stem from a long history of institutionalization to a pattern of failure in foster home settings, poor academic functioning, as well as some form of pathology. Unit A was designed to manage and maintain such hard-to-place youngsters and all resources were mobilized to help the youngsters function in a positive way within the unit structure while placement and long-term planning was worked out.

If a youngster were assigned to Unit B, it was based on an assessment that placement could be secured more quickly and realistically than an assignment to Unit A. Unit B's resources were also organized to manage youngsters effectively and to facilitate long-term planning and placement.

The unit system enabled the child care staff to work more cohesively with the social workers and the clinical team and to focus more sharply on the behavioral problems which children presented whether assigned to either Unit A or B. Weekly staff team meetings in which youngsters were discussed, as well as treatment team meetings which focused on behavior and goals for specific children, helped to give staff a handle on the troubled children with whom they must deal. Thus, the Unit system was the framework which enabled the point system to become operable and effective.

An important aspect of the therapeutic process related to the change in the Residence from a shelter to a Diagnostic Center with the focus on providing an individual assessment and psychosocial plan for each youngster. Subsequently, the psychological and psychiatric staff was increased to provide for a complete diagnostic work-up by both a psychiatrist and psychologist. This diagnostic assessment was followed by a treatment conference which was an interdisciplinary team involving psychological staff, a social worker, a child care worker, a nursing staff and others involved in the care of the children. This team meeting served as a basis of assessment and future planning for the appropriate treatment of each individual child.

It was the responsibility of the social worker to make sure the plans were co-ordinated and to write a psychosocial summary prior to the initial treatment conference and develop long-term plans. A key element of treatment, not only involved the individual counseling given by the social worker, but also group therapy or "rap" sessions. The importance of these sessions were reflected in the fact that as a condition for reaching any level in the point system, a youngster had to attend these groups which were concerned with sharing experiences with other adolescents and reinforcing positive behavior through group interaction. The use of points and group treatment was described by Andrew L. Ross in reference to a day treatment program in Cleveland where youngsters not only received points for coming to group meetings but also by talking in a positive way about group members and confronting each other in a direct way.[9] This concept reinforces the importance of going to group and gives rewards for positive behavior.

Results of Program

The program described above had a great impact upon the adolescents coming into care. The point system made it clear to both staff and residents what the expectations were for both, and the youngsters in the program were able to feel a sense of fairness concerning discipline and rewards for good behavior. Training for the therapeutic program gave staff an insight into the behavior of the youth whom they were now serving and, as results were achieved, staff became increasingly motivated to participate in the process. The point system served to encourage school attendance, better relations toward peer and adults and, most dramatically, decreased the number of absences and runaways by 50%. In many instances, youngsters developed such a strong sense of security and community feeling that they did not want to go into long-term placement although care was taken to find appropriate placements for these youngsters.

The increasing employment of psychological and psychiatric consultants and the emphasis on diagnosis was an improvement in terms of devising an individual treatment plan for each youngster. The individual treatment given by the social worker in counseling and in group interaction helped direct the youngster toward growth and involved the child in the long-term planning for himself or herself. In addition, the assessment and treatment plan helped the child to assist in determining where he or she would go after his or her release or transfer from the Diagnostic Residence.

The change to a unit system from one that divided the population essentially by sex and age was important in terms of dealing with emotionally disturbed youth. It became more beneficial for youngsters and staff to divide units by probable length of stay and aided in working with the child and in the planning. The unit system, while carving out specific boundaries within which to perform, has the capacity to function autonomously. This autonomy gives QSPCC the ability to decentralize its services very quickly. The future availability of sites will, therefore, play a critical role in the Agency's ability to serve adolescents well.

LEVEL	POINTS EARNED	ALLOWANCE	PRIVILEGES
LEVEL ONE	1500	$5.00	AFTERNOON PASS WEEKNIGHT (SPECIAL) ACTIVITY LATE NIGHT T.V.
LEVEL TWO	1000	$2.50	AFTERNOON PASS ONE NIGHT (ONLY) T.V.
LEVEL THREE	100 POINTS OR LESS	$1.00	NONE

CHART I

QSPCC UNIT PROFILES
TABLE OF ORGANIZATION AND FUNCTIONS

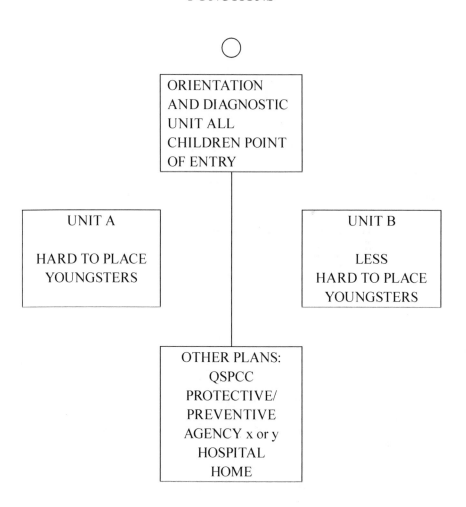

ORIENTATION AND DIAGNOSTIC UNIT ALL CHILDREN POINT OF ENTRY

UNIT A

HARD TO PLACE YOUNGSTERS

UNIT B

LESS HARD TO PLACE YOUNGSTERS

OTHER PLANS: QSPCC PROTECTIVE/ PREVENTIVE AGENCY x or y HOSPITAL HOME

QSPCC UNIT PROFILES
TABLE OF ORGANIZATION
AND FUNCTION

ORIENTATION UNIT
(1-30 DAYS STAY)

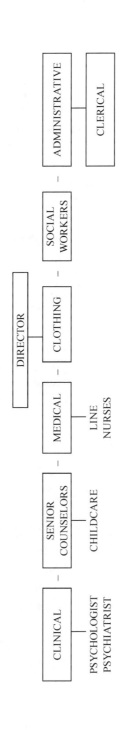

ORIENTATION
UNIT

*

EVALUATE
AND
ASSESS
ALL CHILDREN

*

GOALS

*

MANAGE CALL

DEFINE GOALS

STRUCTURE THE CHILDS
DAY

ARRANGE A
CONTRACTUAL AGREEMENT
WITH THE CHILD'S FAMILY

RE: SHORT TERM PLANS
AND LONG RANGE GOALS

*

SERVICE DELIVERY

*

	INTERDISCIPLINARY TEAMS		
∘ CHILD CARE	∘ UNIT DIRECTOR	∘ PROGRAM PLANNING OFFICER	∘ EXECUTIVE DIRECTOR
∘ SOCIAL SERVICE	∘ NUTRITION		∘ RELIGIOUS EXPERIEN???
∘ EDUCATION	∘ CLOTHING	∘ RESIDENCE DIRECTOR	∘ FICAL AND PERSONNEL
∘ CLINICAL EVALUATIONS	∘ RECREATION	∘ PROTECTIVE/ PREVENTIVE SERVICES	∘ BOARD COMMITTEE
		∘ MEDICAL	RESIDENTIAL CARE

FUNCTIONAL RELATIONSHIPS
AND LINKAGES

*   SHARED INFORMATION

A

┌─────────────────────┐
│ INDIVIDUAL PLAN   │
│ AND   │   B
│ RECOMMENDATION   │
└─────────────────────┘

∨

OTHER

☆ SHARED SERVICES ie ALL UNITS SERVED BY THIS DEPARTMENT

QSPCC UNIT PROFILES
TABLE OF ORGANIZATION AND FUNCTION

UNIT A
(3-5 MONTHS)
SERVING BOYS & GIRLS

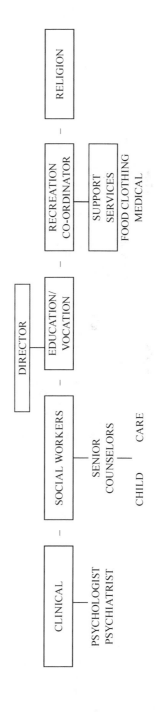

DIRECTOR

| CLINICAL | — | SOCIAL WORKERS | — | EDUCATION/VOCATION | — | RECREATION CO-ORDINATOR | — | RELIGION |

PSYCHOLOGIST
PSYCHIATRIST

SENIOR COUNSELORS

CHILD — CARE

SUPPORT SERVICES
FOOD CLOTHING
MEDICAL

UNIT
A

*

GOAL
FINDING APPROPRIATE PLACEMENT

*

BEHAVIOR
MODIFICATION GROUP
AND
INDIVIDUAL THERAPY

*

SERVICE DELIVERY

*

INTERDISCIPLINARY TEAMS

○ UNIT DIRECTOR
○ MEDICAL
○ RESIDENCE DIRECTOR
○ EXECUTIVE DIRECTOR
○ BOARD COMMITTEE:
○ RESIDENTIAL CARE

○ OFFICER PROGRAM
  PLANNING
○ CLERICAL
○ RELIGIOUS EXPERI???
○ VOLUNTEERS
○ FISCAL PERSONNEL

○ CLINICAL
○ CHILD CARE
○ VOCATIONAL EDUCATION
○ RECREATION
○ NUTRITION

FUNCTIONAL RELATIONSHIPS, INFORMATION SHARING AND LINKING

*

PLACEMENT
OBTAINED

☆ SHARED SERVICES ie ALL UNITS SERVED BY THIS DEPARTMENT

QSPCC UNIT PROFILES

TABLE OF ORGANIZATION AND
FUNCTION

UNIT B
(2-3 MONTHS)
SERVING BOYS & GIRLS

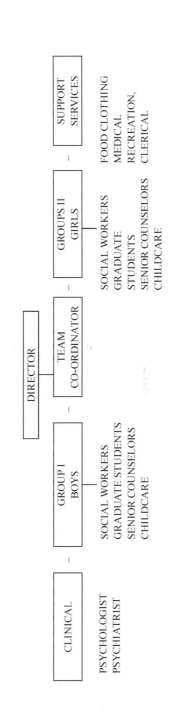

DIRECTOR

TEAM CO-ORDINATOR

CLINICAL
PSYCHOLOGIST
PSYCHIATRIST

GROUP I
BOYS
SOCIAL WORKERS
GRADUATE STUDENTS
SENIOR COUNSELORS
CHILDCARE

GROUPS II
GIRLS
SOCIAL WORKERS
GRADUATE
STUDENTS
SENIOR COUNSELORS
CHILDCARE

SUPPORT
SERVICES
FOOD CLOTHING
MEDICAL
RECREATION,
CLERICAL

```
┌─────────────────────┐
│        UNIT          │
│         B            │
└─────────────────────┘
            *

┌─────────────────────┐
│        FIND          │
│ APPROPRIATE PLACEMENT│
│      (QUICKLY)       │
└─────────────────────┘
            *

┌─────────────────────┐
│  GOAL ATTAINMENT     │
│      SCALE           │
│                      │
│   POINT SYSTEM       │
│                      │
│ GROUP AND INDIVIDUAL │
│      THERAPY         │
└─────────────────────┘
            *

   SERVICE DELIVERY
            *
```

INTERDISCIPLINARY TEAMS

- CLINICAL
- CHILD CARE
- MEDICAL
- SOCIAL SERVICES
- RESIDENCE DIRECTOR

- VOLUNTEERS
- PROTECTIVE/PREVENTIVE SERVICES
- OFFICER PROGRAM PLANNING
- EXECUTIVE DIRECTOR
- RECREATION

- CLERICAL
- NUTRITION
- RELIGIOUS EXPERI???
- UNIT DIRECTOR
- FISCAL PERSONNEL

*

```
PLACEMENT
OBTAINED
```

FUNCTIONAL RELATIONSHIPS, INFORMATION SHARING AND LINKAGES

☆ SHARED SERVICES ie ALL UNITS SERVED BY THIS DEPARTMENT

CHAPTER VIII

The Traditional Unit Model: Advantages and Disadvantages for Child Care Staff

Abstract: From June '70 through August '71, I was a casework supervisor at Children's Village, a residential school for emotionally disturbed boys between the ages of 6 to 13. Subsequently, I was a Unit Director at the above facility from September '71 through September '77.

The following paper, which was published in the Child Care Review, Vol. IV, No. 2, April 1977, reflects my feelings about the unit I administered and the unit system, in general, within the agency. It points out the dichotomy and conflict between social work and child care staff in the area of supervision of child care staff and in the child care staff's struggle for a positive professional identity in a traditional unit model.

The paper was written at a time when the professionalism of child care staff was beginning to be recognized. This emergence from paraprofessional status to professional status was somewhat threatening to social workers, specifically social caseworkers who counseled the children on a regular basis and who met with child care workers on a frequent, usually daily, basis.

Introduction: With the increasing professionalization of child care, there has been an increase of various types of Unit and agency models which have modified the role of the child care counselor. For example, in some residential treatment and child welfare agencies the child care counselor is the focal and primary discipline. All other disciplines may be utilized in auxiliary and consultative roles in relation to the child care staff. In other treatment models, the child care counselor continues to be in an equilateral role in relation to the other professional personnel such as social worker and/or nurse. In other models, the clinical staff is of paramount importance in the treatment of the child and the child care discipline is viewed as subordinate to the clinical role. According to Dr. Hyman Grossbard,

...."One of the perplexing and anxiety-producing questions that plagues the cottage parent today is his self-identity, his role and the place of his cottage vis-a-vis the institution. Confusion about one's identity and home base is one of the most serious sources of anxiety. The cottage parent, particularly in the more progressive and more complex institutions, is frequently unclear as to what his role is and where his responsibilities begin and end.

Traditionally, his role and responsibility were established by common practice, if not by theoretical formulation. Being the only adult within the child's immediate reach, he was the parental surrogate, mentor and disciplinarian. He supposedly created for the child an atmosphere of family life, although at times a dismal one, and transmitted to him the mores and standards of the adult world. The cottage parent's self-image was more or less clear, his authority unchallenged. He was the seat of authority in relation to all of the little things - and big things were rare - that took place within the confines of the institution. Within his cottage, he usually saw himself as an independent sovereign. The front office and the image of the director were invoked or made themselves felt infrequently, in moments of crisis, or in areas outside the immediate life stream of the child."[1]

The cottage parent of today has been deprived of his clear cut self-image. He is no longer sure what he is, what he does and what he represents to the child. He feels no longer related to the total child. The child care counselor is surrounded by a host of people and disciplines - caseworker, psychologist, psychiatrist - dealing with certain facets of the life of the child. His areas of responsibility are still broad, but undelineated. He is not clear about his prerogatives and the areas in which he can exercise his judgment and discretion.

The Unit Model: The model which I am describing is one of four campus models at The Children's Village, a residential treatment center for emotionally disturbed boys between the ages of 7 to 14 years of age in Dobbs Ferry, New York. The unit staff consists of five caseworkers, each of whom is assigned to a specific cottage within the Unit, a Unit Director who supervises the caseworkers and has administrative responsibility for a Unit Psychiatrist, Psychologist and a child care supervisor. The child care supervisor is also the assistant Unit Director who, in addition to assisting the Unit Director in performance of certain administrative functions, also supervises five Senior Counselors, each of whom are child care counselors who are assigned to the five specific cottages within the Unit. Their functions, in addition to the regular child care functions they have been trained to do, consists of supervision of the other child care staff assigned to their respective cottages within the Unit.

Child Care Supervision within this model is done by child care counselors and staff with many years of child care experience. This is in contrast to other models in which supervision of child care staff is done by trained social workers who are categorized as cottage treatment supervisors. This difference in supervision has both a negative and positive effect within the Unit which is under discussion. On the one hand, it perpetuates a conflict in relationships between the social work and child care staff. This has always been a basic problem in this type of model. This conflict is accentuated by virtue of the fact that the caseworkers do not have supervisory responsibility for the child care staff and thus, the child care staff does not feel accountable to the clinical or casework staff in the areas which affect the clinical role. According to Dr. Hyman Grossbard,

"The theoretical base of the respective roles of caseworker and cottage parent has to be clarified with emphasis on the complementary nature of their responsibilities.

At the risk of oversimplification, one may say the cottage parent's area of operation is the immediate reality. He is to present reality as it is; standards and values as they are; a world of structure and organization, with basic parental figures who give and deny, permit and restrain, and with whom the child is to act, interact and grow in the process."[2]

In a positive sense, this traditional model in which there is a clear cut dichotomy between the caseworker and child care staff does tend to strengthen the identity and self-awareness of other child care staff. This factor occurs by virtue of the supervisory process which is maintained by child care personnel and not by the social workers in that the frame of reference is for training child care and not social work staff. This may give the child care worker a sense of continuity and self-awareness while it contains elements of conflict with other staff, primarily the caseworkers who feel that their experience and understanding of childhood pathology would make them the natural supervisors of the child care staff.

Inherent in the dichotomy of this model is the basic question of who 'owns' the child, so to speak. Is it the child care counselor who spends eight or more hours with the child on a daily basis, the social worker who may see the child for only 50 minutes per week or less, or is it the educator or some other staff member?[3] This question tends to raise the issue of the team approach so basic to residential treatment in this era.

The Child Care Counselor and the Team Approach: Within the team concept, no one owns the child. If we look at both the caseworker and the child care counselor as two integral members of the team, we must recognize that they subscribe to the same values and aim toward the same objectives. They differ only in their areas of operation and in the array of techniques employed. "Total environmental management implies a team approach embracing a variety of disciplines."[4] In a paper on the child care worker compiled by members of the American Association for Children's Residential Centers, it was expressed that ... "not only is the distribution of their disciplines unequal, but within the disciplinary hierarchy child care has been accorded the least recognition and the lowest status."[5]

This is not true within this model as heretofore described in that the status of the senior child care counselor, with the various responsibilities which this role entails, has been given formalized recognition by the total agency and certainly prior informal recognition by the Unit administration. The administration recognizes that the child care staff under the supervision of trained, practicing child care counselors, i.e., Senior Counselors, affects the child care staff in a positive sense in that they have some feeling of identity and carry some authority and power in the decision-making which exists within the team approach.

Conclusion: The traditional model in which there is a clear dichotomy between clinical and child care staff accentuates the conflict between both child care and social work although the team approach is viewed as essential in treating children. The competition between both disciplines as to who owns the child can be dissipated somewhat if there is a clear recognition that both caseworkers and child care counselors subscribe to the same values and aim toward the same objectives. They differ only in their areas of operation and in the array of techniques employed.

The supervision of child care staff, if done by child care practitioners, enhances the identity of and the authority of child care staff providing the administration allows the child care staff to be involved in decision-making processes within the team. However, child care supervision, if maintained in the hands solely of child care staff, only accentuates the conflict and competition with the clinical staff, i.e. social workers, etc. who feel that their experiences and understanding of childhood pathology would make them the natural supervisors of the child care staff.

CHAPTER IX

Stimuli and Milieu Therapy in a Geriatric Setting

Abstract: In December '67, I was the social service supervisor at Daughters of Jacob Geriatric Center in the South Bronx. Several months after my assignment at the facility, I was assigned to Ward 4B, a ward for frail and infirm female patients from 80 to 98 years of age, in order to implement comprehensive social services to all of the patients of the ward. The details of that assignment are in the following paper. It indicates that elderly, frail, infirm, and bedridden patients can be helped by a multidisciplinary approach, to function more effectively and respond more appropriately to their surroundings. It was the purpose of this project to demonstrate the possibility that the development of an optimal therapeutic milieu on a chronic hospital ward for deteriorated geriatric patients can decelerate the deterioration process and stimulate responsiveness and outer-directed interests on the part of the patients.

Introduction: In December of 1967, I was assigned to Ward 4B, located in the Hospital Division of Daughters of Jacob Geriatric Center, to provide comprehensive social services to all of the patients on the ward. This step signaled a change from the traditional assignment of patient caseloads wherein workers carried ongoing cases that had been originally assigned to them regardless of the location of the case in the hospital or home.

It was the purpose of this project to demonstrate the possibility that the development of an optimal therapeutic milieu on a chronic hospital ward for deteriorated geriatric patients can decelerate the deterioration process and stimulate responsiveness and outer-directed interests on the part of the patients. An optimal milieu is one in which at least the following is provided for:

(1) Adequate medical, nursing, and physical care.
(2) Comprehensive social services wherein at least one trained worker (or a team) provides group and casework services to patients and families.
(3) A varied, stimulating program of recreational and occupational therapy.
(4) Close staff teamwork including regular ward conferences with all relevant staff; i.e. physicians, psychiatrists, nurses, social workers, physiotherapists, occupational and recreational therapists, volunteer director, etc.
(5) High staff morale and staff interest in the welfare of all patients.
(6) Pleasant physical surroundings including sufficient space for programming and socializing and abundant sensor stimulants; i.e. plants, colorful curtains, pictures, etc.
(7) Specialized programs for the handicapped.
(8) An organized daily program of music, art and recreation with as much involvement as possible of family and volunteers with patients.

While traditional explanations of senility rely heavily on the organic deterioration in older people, there have been significant efforts to investigate the environment as a contribution factor. Anderson (1963) distinguished the effects of immediate environment from the effects of past experience; three dimensions of the immediate environment were suggested by him for study: stimulation patterns, incentives and modes of control.[1]

Catti (1963) suggested that there is a direct linkage between organic deterioration and the effects of the environment.

"Living without the stimulating input of meaningful and repeated human interaction results in psychologically regressive and physiologically degenerative processes. Integrated activity of the complex neural processes of the brain depends upon a variation in the sensory environment."[2]

Catti pointed to a parallel between the sensory deprivation experiments conducted with young adults and the effects of decreased input on the aging. Heron (1957) found there to be deleterious effects from prolonged exposure to a rigidly monotonous environment: the thinking of these young adults became impaired, childish emotional responses were demonstrated, visual perception became disturbed, and there was a good deal of reminiscence.[3]

The following project is somewhat similar to those described in that observations were made of the effects of a variety of interventions. However, attention here is focused on a much older age group whose responsiveness to any kind of intervention has not been demonstrated and is generally considered unlikely. The present study will attempt to (1) develop and evaluate both qualitatively and quantitatively the effects on the cognitive, affective, and social functioning of older "senile" patients of a program of increased social, psychological, and physical stimulation including response facilitation; and (2) make specific recommendations based on these findings. This program was initiated in the winter of 1967-'68.

Description of Ward 4B

Ward 4B was an open ward of female patients ranging in age from 80 to 98 years of age within the Hospital Division of the Daughters of Jacob Geriatric Center located in the South Bronx of New York City.

Before we describe Ward 4B, let us first describe more fully the institutional setting in which this project was developed. Daughters of Jacob is an established 500 bed institution which cares for both chronically ill and healthy male and female geriatric populations. It was established in 1894 and is a member of the Federation of Jewish Philanthropies and accredited by the Joint Commission of Accreditation of Hospitals. It has a staff of about 450 and boasts of a one-to-one patient to staff ratio.

The building complex of the Center is composed of (1) Domiciliary or Home Division which admits individuals who are unable to function independently in the community but are sufficiently well to care for their own needs; and (2) the Home Division which admits those who are too infirm to be served in the Domiciliary Division. Most of the population of the Hospital is over 80 years of age.

It is within this setting that Ward 4B is located with its patients who were in various stages of physical and mental deterioration and, as a whole, comprised one of the most regressed groups in the Institution. Fourteen of the patients on the ward were being studied for the purpose of continuity. Two of them were blind, one was severely deaf, at least six were severely disoriented and confused. There were no critically ill patients although all patients were physically limited to some degree. Most of the patients needed assistance in their personal care. All of them responded to staff in varying degrees but all suffered severe limitations in intra-group relations. Most of the studied population were visited by friends and family whose main concerns were for the patients' physical care and comfort.

The program which had been in operation on Ward 4B prior to my assignment had been one characterized by very high standards of medical and nursing care, well prepared and supervised diets, and thorough housekeeping. Psychiatric care had been minimal. The occupational therapist had been involved on the ward once a week and the Group Work Department had planned a program of recreational activities on a daily basis for all patients on Ward 4B, and for those who could ambulate towards activities outside of the ward. This was prior to the recreational therapist's involvement as the recreation group worker on Ward 4B.

However, as stated heretofore, a number of trained and untrained social workers were assigned to patients on the ward with no access to the medical record. Teamwork among the staff was either non-existent or very informal. There were no team or ward conferences on a regular basis or sensitivity training of staff.

Expanded Services of the Demonstration Project

It had been the hope of staff assigned to Ward 4B to make innovations, expand and intensify present services in order that the aforementioned minimal requirements of a therapeutic milieu for a geriatric ward could be provided. It seemed at the time that this hope could be realized. While regular staff ward meetings had not been organized, I had met with medical, nursing, administrative, group work, volunteer and recreational staff.

The first task was to attune staff to the variety of psychological and social needs of the patients, and to encourage as much communication as possible among different levels of staff and between staff and patients.[4] A weekly team meeting was organized for these purposes. All staff on the ward were asked to attend: physicians, nurses, aides, social workers, recreational and occupational therapists and volunteers. Each staff member was asked to keep ongoing records on each patient and to share these records with each other. Each staff member was asked to keep ongoing records on each patient and to share these records with each other. Each patient was discussed from an historical, social, psychological and physical viewpoint. It became apparent as the meetings progressed that the major focus shifted from the work of the professional staff to that of the nurses aides. Assigned to feed, clean, clothe and generally care for the patients, their relationships became an important source of information and an important focus of therapeutic intervention.

All staff members participated in the following program plan which evolved over a period of five months. More intense and varied stimulation (tactile, auditory, visual and gustatory) was sought in the physical, social and psychological spheres.[5] It had been the hope of staff assigned to Ward 4B to make innovations, expand and intensify services in order that the aforementioned minimal requirements of a therapeutic milieu for a geriatric ward could be provided for. It seemed at the time that this hope was being realized. While regular staff ward meetings had not been organized, I met with the medical, nursing, group work and volunteer administration.

On the ward, there was a daily program. On Monday, there was recorded music with rhythmic accents. On Tuesday, the recreation worker showed the patients pictures of objects of varied subject matter. On Wednesday, short films of assorted subjects were shown in the ward on a portable screen. In addition, there was a live musical program. On Thursday, volunteer beauty aides worked with the patients around make-up and grooming. On Friday, there was another live music program in which I played the piano and the recreational therapist accompanied me on the guitar. The patients were served a small cup of wine during a recreation program three afternoons a week. To avoid routinization, variety and change were constantly introduced into each of these daily programs, always keeping in mind the importance of stimulating the senses. Two very successful programs included the use of balloons and the introduction of individual plants for each bedside. The social worker was in almost daily contact with the patients and their families. I worked with them around both their emotional and concrete problems and I was allowed to insert important psychosocial information in the medical charts.

We hoped to develop a high-powered volunteer program with the Beth Jacob School for Girls in the Fall of '68. A meeting had been held with the supervisor of the volunteer program and some of the girls involved. The girls who attended were quite impressed and all had expressed a desire to work at Daughters of Jacob in the Fall of '68.

In addition, we initiated and developed group meetings with four nurses' aides regularly assigned to Ward 4B. These weekly meetings, organized by the Director of Nursing, Mrs. Dow, were led by the consultant to the Social Work Department, Mrs. Silverstone, for the purpose of exploring the attitudes of staff and recognizing their feelings and problems in the hope of enhancing the morale of the aides and in turn sensitizing their reactions to the patients. The aides were seen as having the most intense and intimate contact with the patients and greatly in need of recognition, support and expression of feeling about their work.

Program Observations

After several months, we made several observations of the effects of the program to date. We noticed that patients were now going out of the ward to take part in programs in the sitting room on the fourth floor, and that the level of interest and participation in all programs was considerably higher. Whereas previously the patients had reacted to the program with only polite tolerance there seemed now to be definitely a spirit of cooperation with patients who openly looked forward to each daily program.

The most widely reported therapeutic approach based on the philosophy that environment and experience can be as important as biology on the aging process is that of milieu therapy. This therapy is based on the treatment philosophy that when the environment lacks stimulus for the aging, stimulus must be provided.[6] Of course, there were many problems which we faced. Even the best programs conducted on a half hour basis each day cannot nullify or counterbalance a whole day of boredom, irritating routines, and physical and mental deterioration which prevails in an open ward such as 4B. In other words, we were faced with a dehumanizing environment in our efforts toward achieving a therapeutic milieu. However, we felt that an important first step toward this goal would be to stabilize the ward. Prior to this program, there had been too many patients moved in and out of Ward 4B. Too often there had been twenty occupied beds in the ward which certainly made for a rather crowded situation. Thus we attempted to change the density of the population and provide a living room atmosphere. We obtained a table, flowers, chairs, a shelf for magazines, pictures, a calendar, etc. It brought about some incentive for the ambulatory patients to leave their bedside, associate with others and provide some interest on a daily basis. Even for the completely bedbound patients these milieu changes gave them an incentive to try and get better. We felt that even those patients who were blind and therefore could not see the changes were affected positively by the milieu transition.

As mentioned heretofore, only 14 of the patients in Ward 4B were included in the study. Detailed notes were being kept on each of these 14 patients and in addition their progress, lack of progress and/or deterioration were being charted monthly according to the patients' ability to care independently for themselves in regard to eating, toilet habits, their level of social interaction and changes in their medical condition.

Implications: It was hoped that enough information would be gathered and observations made that an optimal therapeutic milieu could be extended to other hospital wards and that a formal research project in which genuine tasks would be carried out could be instituted and indeed, this is what subsequently occurred.

One of the most significant implications of the results of this study is that sensory deprivation related to an institutionalized environment, even with the best medical and sanitary conditions, is detrimental to the overall functioning of the senile aged. According to Loew and Silverstone, "intensified sensory input, on the other hand, produces 1) increased affective states and 2) stimulation of social behavior in the direction of a desire for some sort of change. If these two factors are thought of in terms of a resultant increment in general excitation, then one must consider the function which this drive serves."[7] It is imperative that some activity commensurate with the abilities and limitations of individuals, be provided in order to channel the increased energy. This may be accomplished by grading patients on some criterion for different programs at different levels. Probably the most beneficial service can be provided by separating individuals into different groups according to ability and potential and their applying select programs based on those group abilities. Thus, homogeneous groups may be established, each with similar rehabilitation potential and needs. Differential rehabilitation programs, medical or psychological, can then be developed. It has been reported that even severely brain-damaged patients respond in an artificial milieu with well-planned programs for orientation activities and socialization.[8] To be avoided for the very elderly patient, regardless of his or her ability and potential, are monotonous routinization, depersonalization, blandness, sterility, and infantilization. To be encouraged are a variety of meaningful inputs besides that of feeding and caring.

CHAPTER X

Conclusion: An Ecosystems Concept in the Practice of Social Work

Abstract: The following paper attempts to summarize the previous papers and to point out a direction of practice for the social work practitioner. Its premise is that social work has to deal with its own cognitive restructuring and view social phenomena as they are and not as social workers would want them to be to suit their interests in particular methods. Direct social work practice can no longer be defined only through the personal encounters of worker and client. The paper emphasizes the need for workers to be opened to an infinite variety of interventions. It is this author's contention that with an open system of thought and a realistic confrontation with life as it is, direct practice in social work will adapt and survive.

Introduction: The papers which are presented in this Independent Study Project reflect eighteen years of social work experience in various agencies and programs. They represent, essentially, a variety of treatment models and concepts which have been applied to various client populations from children to the aged. The essential commonality of these models is in their emphasis on a team approach and in the need for a treatment frame of reference in order to effectively serve a client population.

What we are looking at are systems and models of treatment - a family system's approach, i.e. incest, milieu therapy approach, i.e. Chapters VI, VII, VIII, a multidisciplinary approach, i.e. focusing on and treating criminal and deviant behavior; advocacy and direct service model, i.e. domestic violence, Chapter II; a parent training and self-help model, Chapter III and finally a preventive treatment approach which is holistic as well, as described in Chapter V. These systems are effective and have resulted in positive change, but there have been problems inherent in their implementation. For example, while the impact of stimuli therapy and milieu change were effective, it did cause agitation from both some patients and nursing staff at the geriatric center. The Ward 4B experiment worked and was subsequently transferred to other wards. When individual patients began to reveal a desire to dress and go into programs outside of the ward program, nursing and medical staff were not fully prepared to handle this. The status quo was affected. Schedules and work activities were disrupted. Thus there were complaints. The push to maintain the status quo was as strong as the pull to change it. Hence new conflicts and problems had arisen as a result of our efforts to improve the functioning of the patients.

In maintaining a traditional model at Children's Village, we only accentuated conflict between social worker and child care staff. Consequently, this model was modified and at the time that I left the agency, the caseworkers were assigned to the cottages as cottage supervisors. The problem now was that the authority of the child care senior counselors was again diluted.

In order to effectuate a strong preventive family approach we had to work closely with other agencies in the community. Please refer to Chapter IV. The philosophy was Holistic - focusing on the environment and the social, biological and economic variables which impinged on the clients we served. The expulsive phenomena which was ubiquitous in most families which led to the placement of children was not simply an intrapsychic phenomena but rather, an interpsychic one which included environmental factors. To work within the framework of individual or family counseling alone would have to be self-defeating. Consequently, we offered the community surrounding TIP such services as working with social action groups, teen mothers' groups and consultation with tenant associations. We also were active in such network systems as the Teen Pregnancy Network and the Bronx Task Force on Child Abuse and Neglect. These factors helped us to survive. Nevertheless the politics of funding modified any grandiose goals in that cash flow was always a problem and all programs which were funded had to be budgeted extremely carefully in order not to lose monies. Thus "success" brings with it its own set of problems.

However, as I see it, the essential goal of therapy or casework or counseling is not to establish principles of behavior, but rather to apply established principles to achieve behavioral change.[1] If one views developments in the mental health field over the last several decades, a progression toward broader and broader views of etiology and treatment of emotionally disturbed and mentally ill and dysfunctional individuals and families are clearly evident. The focus of the psychoanalyst, the non-directive therapist, the clinical social work psychotherapist, and to a great extent, even the behaviorally-oriented therapist, is on the individual. The growth of family treatment approaches has widened the view of the mental health profession considerably. Family therapists have, in recent years, broadened their perspective beyond the nuclear family. Speck's (1967) network approach is an example.[2] Auserwald (1968) has gone even further in his ecological approach by focusing on the context of the community.[3] Community mental health practitioners have gone even further by shifting the emphasis of interventions from the individual or family to community agencies and institutions. Saranson (1976)[4] and Klein (1968)[5] have even disputed the significance of individual influences on behavior.

These different paradigms are often in apparent conflict. Howells (1971), a family therapist, for example, states the proposition that:

"Individual psychiatry ... taking the adults as the functional unit, the child as the functional unit, or the adolescent as the functional unit, is obsolete. Individual psychiatry is replaced by family psychiatry."[6]

Klein (1968), a community psychologist, reaches another seemingly contradictory conclusion:

"I have come to believe that the community represents the single most important social matrix which man has invented and that it is only in this matrix that the concept of mental health can be developed most fruitfully."[7]

These competing theories place today's clinician in a rather confusing position. If one chooses to be eclectic, how are the competing theories reconciled?

The Ecosystems Approach: The process of synthesis is facilitated by what we call the ecosystems approach to understanding emotional disturbance, deviant behavior and dysfunction.[8] The perspective draws heavily from the science of ecology, that is, the study of the relationship between man and his environment.

The ecological perspective and its relationship in therapeutic change serves as the basis for this Independent Study Project. It represents an attempt to go beyond the paradigms of the individual approach, the family approach, and the community approach, to a paradigm or model which allows the social worker to function in the total ecological system.

It is my contention that the ecological system is modified by the philosophy, mission and purpose of the agency or facility in which the worker is employed and by the clients which the agency serves. Thus the worker must be able to utilize those systems, which are relevant to the treatment of his clients. For example, in order to develop an effective model of treatment within the Incest Treatment Unit at Queensboro Society for the Prevention of Cruelty to Children the workers and the supervisor had to be able to work closely with the court system in order to develop leverage in working with the perpetrators and, indeed, the other members of the families in which incest occurred. It was the Family Court's demand that treatment be implemented which enabled the workers to successfully treat the perpetrators as well as their families, for without the court backing, there would be massive denial and even greater resistance to therapy. In addition, the Family Court usually enabled the Unit to work more effectively with the perpetrator by initially separating him from the family constellation. He had to find a place to stay and remain outside of the home unless treatment recommendations stated otherwise.

In addition to the Family Court System, the worker had to work closely with the Child Welfare System from which referrals were made. Without their cooperation and input, the Unit could not be productive.

The treatment model itself was eclectic and pragmatic. It had to be linked to these two other systems, the court and child welfare, in order to survive and function effectively. Each system is an independent entity, yet each is a part of the total environment and interacts with and affects all other systems within the ecosystem.[9] Additionally, it is assumed that each system functions under general systems theory laws governing open systems. These laws define an open system as having the ability to 1) obtain input from the environment; 2) maintain a certain form and structure which makes up the system; 3) grow and develop a more differentiated structure; and 4) produce output which can affect its environment. It is my belief that to make major changes in systems, be they at the intrapsychic, family or community level, requires radical restructuring of the system. It is a major hypothesis of this approach that such restructuring is only possible after the system has been placed under a sufficient degree of stress so as to break down the system's homeostatic mechanism, and to essentially disorganize the system. This process is a description of a crisis framed in system theory terms. Thus, to rephrase the hypothesis, significant change requires the occurrence of crisis or severe dysfunction.

Summary of Observations

Social workers, whether they work in a geriatric setting or a residential school for emotionally disturbed children or a community based agency such as a neighborhood house are essentially agents of change and have to effectuate positive, therapeutic change for their clients within the systems they have developed or under which they work. During the 18 years of experience which this project covers, I had the opportunity to work in various systems and to help to develop others. It would seem to me that whenever changes occurred which threatened the primary balance or homeostasis of an existing system then resistance to change was greatest. However, if there was a serious dysfunctional situation in a community, for example, no resources were able to reduce those pathological conditions, then change could be more easily implemented such as the development of a family services program within TIP Neighborhood House, which is located within a community with severe socio-economic problems. Once approval for a program was granted other services would eventually be developed such as a parents' anonymous self-help group, a domestic violence program and a teen mothers' group.

We can also see that within a short-term facility for severely disturbed, acting-out adolescents such as existed at QSPCC, a unit system was developed with little resistance from staff who responded to the crisis of overcrowded conditions in the facility. As a result of this system, the following occurred:

1. There was a reduction in AWOL's.
2. There was a reduction in vandalism.
3. Youngsters developed a strong sense of security and communal feeling which affected their desire to go into other facilities.
4. School attendance increased.
5. Fighting and cursing among peers decreased.
6. Staff morale improved.
7. Residential recreational programs improved.
8. Behavioral improvement in the facility[10] was carried over on home visits.

The implementation of new programs was more difficult to achieve when a structure had been in operation over a long period of time such as at Daughters of Jacob Geriatric Center and the Children's Village.

Empirically speaking, whether resistance to innovation and change is great or mild within an agency or facility, the populace whom the social worker serves is effected. If the individual is viewed as a complete entity with bio-psycho-social needs and if a comprehensive approach is implemented to meet those needs, the individual has a greater chance to develop a positive therapeutic modification in his intra and interpsychic systems.

Conclusion: According to Carol Meyer, "The distinction between systems thinking and methods has to be clarified. Once again, conceptual apples and oranges are being confused. The ecosystems perspective allows social workers to look at psychosocial phenomena, account for complex variables, assess the dynamic interplay of these variables, draw conceptual boundaries around the unit of attention or the case, and then generate ideas for interventions. At this point, methodology enters in, for in any particular case - meaning a particular individual, family, group, institutional unit, or geographical area - any number of interventions might be needed."[11]

This formulation demonstrates that the methodological proliferations in the profession can come together under a conceptual umbrella. The first professional obligation is to assume responsibility for exploring and accumulating data about the unit of attention as it is defined by law, agency sanction, community or client interest, or natural or physical boundaries. Then the most complex professional skill of all must be called into play: that of assessment. This is the intellectual process of determining with the client, in whatever form - individual, family, group, or community - and on the basis of social work knowledge and judgment, exactly what has to be done in this situation. Now social work's rich repertoire is available for selective use. The possibilities range from implementation of housing policy to treatment of an individual.

This perspective - actually a model of practice when methodology is included - allows for social work's differences while being accountable to whatever sector of social problems social workers assign themselves or for which they are responsible. This model allows for prevention and treatment, for all modalities, and for techniques that have yet to be invented. No client gets left out, and all social workers engaged in professional practice gain the opportunity to do "their thing" flexibly and creatively.

Direct social work practice can no longer be defined only through the personal encounters of worker and client.[12] Historically, social workers have worked in an institutional framework, thus accounting for their relationships to clients in certain contexts, as in hospitals, residential schools for disturbed youth, neighborhood centers and treatment facilities for a whole range of disturbances and developmental disabilities, the work place, welfare departments, schools, and the primary social work institution of family and children's services. These settings, in different configurations, have been conceptualized as fields of social work practice which have been called health, mental health, justice, education, economics and family, adult, and child development.[13] Now, having been given or having assumed responsibility for working with people in these sectors, the time has arrived when the profession is held accountable for its work.

Even assuming that its practice is psychotherapy or behavior modification or psychosocial treatment or problem-solving or task-centered practice or family treatment or group work, none of these methods, either individually or combined, provides a conceptualization of the arena for which social work is expected to be accountable. In fact, any or all of those methods can be identified in other helping professions such as psychology, psychiatry, and nursing. It seems that by now, over sixty years after the beginning of its professionalization, social work should be able to assert its established expertise in defined arenas shaped by fields of practice, and no longer be restricted to methodology as the way to identify itself. This idea - that social work has an arena for which it might be accountable - is the basis for shifting from a methodological orientation to an ecosystems or an epidemiological orientation, which provides another alternative for the purposes of practice.

How is this way of thinking about practice different from past ways of thinking, and what is involved in an epidemiological orientation? By thinking hospital floor, for example, rather than twenty cases, or by drawing a boundary around an arena, certain phenomena, or conditions of life, the related variables within this boundary can be explored and assessed, and whatever methodology or model of practice suits the defined need in front of us can be chosen. Where does the boundary come from? Who decides where to draw it? The answer is the familiar social worker's response,

"It depends." Sometimes, the area enclosed by the boundary is a predetermined catchment area in a community mental health center or a prison yard in a maximum security correction facility for violent offenders or a floor in a hospital. Sometimes it is a geographical area defined in accordance with a practice approach, and how the boundary is drawn makes a difference to the practice.

In child welfare, for example, a boundary might be drawn around a certain number of city blocks or, in rural areas, around a certain number of square miles. Within that area, all the components of child welfare transactions would be located - natural parents, child, foster parents, group home, crash pad, counseling center, homemaker service, day care center, administrative office, and so on.

Boundaries can also be drawn around neighborhoods to determine who and what have an impact on the client in his or her environment, so that the social worker can influence the environment to help the client cope better.[14] Geographical or conceptual boundaries can be drawn for all kinds of purposes, whether to suit the requirements of law or practice. Attention to the many events, people and influences within whatever arena social workers have defined as theirs will virtually push them into doing something about what they find. Epidemiology is concerned with the incidence and distribution of disease in the case of public health, but in the case of social work it is concerned with the incidence and distribution of psychosocial adaptations. "Drawing boundaries is a conceptual skill, and the conditions and needs of people within the boundaries that social workers devise will be made so conspicuous that it will be impossible to ignore their idiosyncratic requirements for intervention."[15]

This formulation defines social work practice broadly and makes it impossible to limit social work to whatever method workers happen to know. Practice includes the application of intellectual and assessment skills necessary to understand the dynamics of the social work arena, and indeed, to individualize need for a range of services.[16] For example, in thinking <u>hospital floor,</u> a social worker will notice things not observed in individual cases, such as the relationship of patients to each other and to visiting relatives, the impact of hospital personnel, the atmosphere of the hospital, the isolation of patients from the outside world, and so on. Without question, such a "case" will demand more varied intervention than would the use of the professional relationship alone.

Social workers have but begun to create the interventions that are possible. With an open system of thought and a realistic confrontation with life as it is, direct practice in social work will adapt and survive. "Despite the politicians who have denigrated social work services, despite the taxpayers' misconceptions that social work is only for others, not for them, despite social work's crisis of confidence, social workers can make the choice to have a future."[17]

BIBLIOGRAPHY

Preface

Carlton, T.O. and Jung, M., "Adjustment or Change: Attitudes Among Social Workers", Social Work, Vol. 17, No. 5, November 1972.

Chapter I

Bartlett, Harriet, The Common Base of Social Work Practice, New York: National Association of Social Workers, 1970.

Meyer, Carol H., "What Directions for Direct Practice?", Social Work, Vol. 24, No. 4, July 1979.

Mullen, Edward J. and Dumpson, James R., eds., Evaluation of Social Intervention, San Francisco: Jersey-Bass, 1976.

Richmond, Mary, What Is Social Casework? New York: Russell Sage Foundation, 1922.

Chapter II

Bandura, Albert and Walters, Richard H., Adolescent Aggression, New York: Ronald Press, 1959.

Burnbaum, David, "New York is Found Safest of 13 Cities in Crime Study", The New York Times, April 15, 1974, p. 1.

Cohen, Albert K. Deviance and Control, Englewood Cliffs, New Jersey: Prentice-Hall, 1966.

Durkheim, Emile, Suicide: A Study in Sociology, translated. John A. Spaulding and George Simpson, New York: Free Press, 1951.

Ennis, Philip H., "Crimes, Victims and Police", Transaction, Vol. 4, 1967, pp. 36-44.

Gibbons, Donald C. and Jones, Joseph R., The Study of Deviance, Englewood Cliffs, New Jersey: Prentice-Hall, 1975.

Glassner, Barry and Freedman, Jonathan A., Clinical Sociology, New York and London: Longman Inc., 1979.

Hernstein, Richard J. and Wilson, James Q., "Are Criminals Made or Born?" The New York Times Magazine, August 4, 1985, p. 31.

Hirschi, Travis, Causes of Delinquency, Berkeley: University of California Press, 1971.

Levine, James P., "The Potential for Crime Overreporting in Criminal Victimization Surveys", Criminology, Vol. 14, No. 3, November 1976, pp. 307-330.

Lewis, Michael, "Culture and Gender Roles: There's No Unisex in the Nursery", Psychology Today, Vol. 5, May 1972, pp. 54-57.

Light, Donald Jr. and Keller, Suzanne, Sociology, 2nd Ed., New York: Alfred H. Knopf, 1979.

McGee, Reece, Ed. Sociology: An Introduction, New York: Holt, Rinehart & Winston, 1980.

Merton, Robert K., Social Theory and Social Structure, Glencoe, Illinois: Free Press, 1957.

Miller, Walter B., "Lower-Class Culture as a Generating Milieu of Gang Delinquency", Journal of Sociological Issues, Vol. 14, 1958, pp. 5-19.

Robbins, Lewis, "Traditional Reductionism Is Unsatisfactory", International Journal of Psychiatry, Vol. 7, No. 2, 1969.

Shaw, Clifford R. and McKay, Henry D., Delinquency Areas, Chicago: University of Chicago Press, 1929.

Sutherland, Edwin H., "Differential Association", in Wolfgang, Savity & Johnston, Eds., The Sociology of Crime and Delinquency, Vol. 14, No. 3, 1958.

Sutherland, Edwin H. and Cressy, Donald R., Principles of Criminology, 6ᵗʰ ed., Philadelphia: Lippincott, 1960.

"Uniform Crime Reports", Crime in the United States, 1975, Washington, D.C.: U.S. Government Printing Office, 1976.

"Wide Disparities in Crime Totals Found in Sampling of 8 Cities", The New York Times, January 27, 1974, p. 34.

Williams, Jay R. and Gold, Martin, "From Delinquent Behavior to Official Delinquency", Social Problems, Vol. 20 (Fall 1972), pp. 209-229.

Chapter III

Carlson, Bonnie E., "Battered Women and Their Assailants", Social Work, November 1977, pp. 455-460.

Cook, David R. and Frantz-Cook, Anne, "A Systemic Treatment Approach to Wife Battering", Journal of Marital and Family Therapy, 1984, Vol. 10, pp. 83-93.

Costantino, Cathy, "Intervention with Battered Women: The Lawyer-Social Worker Team", Social Work, Vol. 26, November '81, pp. 456-460.

Kettrell, Willis and Mohl, Allan, A Needs Assessment of Community District 6 in the South Bronx; TIP Neighborhood House, Inc.: April 1981 (unpublished).

Margolin, G., "Conjoint Marital Therapy to Enhance Anger Management and Reduce Spouse Abuse", American Journal of Family Therapy, Vol. 7, 1981, pp. 675-692.

McShane, Claudette, "Community Services for Battered Women", Social Work, Vol. 21, January 1979, pp. 34-39.

Pfouts, Jane H. and Renz, Connie, "The Future of Wife Abuse Programs", Social Work, Vol. 25, November '81, pp. 451-455.

Reynolds, Rosemary and Siegle, Else, "A Study of Casework with Sadomasochistic Marriage Partners", Social Casework, Vol. 40, December 1959, pp. 545-551.

Chapter IV

Carkhuff, Robert R. and Berenson, Bernard G., Beyond Counseling and Therapy, New York: Holt, Rinehart & Winston, 1967.

Gordon, Thomas, P.E.T. Parent Effectiveness Training: The Tested New Way to Raise Responsible Children, New York: The New American Library, Inc., 1975.

Rogers, Carl, "The Necessary and Sufficient Conditions of Therapeutic Personality Change", Journal of Consulting Psychology, Vol. 22, March '57, pp. 95-103.

Therrien, Mark E., "Evaluating Empathy Skill Training for Parents", Social Work, Vol. 24, September '79, pp. 417-419.

Vattano, Anthony J., "Power to the People: Self-help Groups", Social Work, Vol. 17, July 1972, pp. 7-15.

Chapter V

Child Welfare Information Services (CWIS) Print Out Sheet, New York State Department of Social Services: Albany, New York, 1980.

Kettrell, Willis and Mohl, Allan, Needs Assessment of Community District 6 In The South Bronx, TIP Neighborhood House, Inc., April 1981 (unpublished).

Chapter VI

Brant, Renee and Tisca, Veronica, "The Sexually Misused Child", American Journal of Orthopsychiatry, Vol. 47, Jan. 1977, pp. 80-90.

Brooks, Barbara, Familial Influences in Father-Daughter Incest, New York Hospital - Cornell Medical Center, White Plains, New York.

DeFrances, Vincent, Protecting the Child Victim of Sex Crimes Committed by Adults. Denver, Colorado: American Humane Association, 1969.

Giarretto, Henry, "Humanistic Treatment of Father-Daughter Incest", Child Abuse and Neglect - The Family and The Community, Eds. R.E. Helfer and C.H. Kempe, Michigan State University: Ballinger Publications, 1977.

Mohl, Allan, MSS, A Comparison Study of Three Treatment Models in Dealing with Intra-Familial Child Sexual Abuse (Mimeo), QSPCC, Jamaica, Queens, 1980.

Sgroi, Suzanne, Ed.D., "The Sexual Assault of Children, Dynamics of the Problem and Abuses in Program Development", Sexual Abuse of Children: Implications From the Sexual Trauma Treatment Program of Connecticut, Community Council of Greater New York, April 1979.

Shamroy, Jerilyn A., "A Perspective on Childhood Sexual Abuse", Social Work, Vol. 25, March 1980, pp. 128-131.

"Attacking the Last Taboo", Time Magazine, April 14, 1980, p. 72.

Zaphiris, Alexander G., Ed.D., Incest: The Family with Two Known Victims, Englewood, Colorado: American Humane Association, 1978.

Chapter VII

Keith-Lucas, Alan and Sanford, Clifford, W., Group Child Care as a Family Service, Chapel Hill: University of North Carolina Press, 1977.

Meyer, Margrit, Odom, E.E. and Wax, Bernice S., "Birth and Life of an Incentive System in a Residential Institution for Adolescents", Child Welfare, October 1973.

Ross, Andrew L., "Combining Behavior Modification and Group Work Techniques in a Day Treatment Center", Child Welfare, July 1974.

Schaefer, Charles E., "Some Guidelines on the Effective Use of Punishment", Child Care Quarterly, Vol. 5, No. 4, Winter 1976.

Warm, Harriet L., "Planning in a Public Child Welfare Agency: A Case Study", Child Welfare, February 1978.

Chapter VIII

American Association for Children's Residential Centers, From Chaos to Order: A Collective View of the Residential Treatment of Children, New York: Child Welfare League of America, Inc., 1972.

Beker, Jerome, "Editorial: On Defining the Child Care Profession", Child Care Quarterly, Vol. 5, No. 3, 1976, pp. 165-166.

Grossbard, Hyman, Cottage Parents - What they Have to Be, Know and Do, New York: Child Welfare League of America, 1960.

Chapter IX

Anderson, J.E., "Environment and Meaningful Activity", in Williams, Tibbett and Donahue, Eds., Processes of the Aging, Vol. 1, New York: Atherton Press, 1963, pp. 223-244.

Berkman, Barbara, "Mental Health and the Aging: A Review of the Literature for Clinical Social Workers", Clinical Social Work Journal, Vol. 6, No. 3, 1978, pp. 230-249.

Butler, R.N., "Psychiatry and the Elderly: An Overview", The American Journal of Psychiatry, Vol. 132, No. 9, 1975, pp. 893-900.

Cath, S.H., "Some Dynamics of Middle and Later Years", Smith College Studies in Social Work, Vol. 33, February 1963, pp. 121-124.

Heron, W., "The Pathology of Boredom", in Coopersmith, S. (Ed.), Frontiers of Psychological Research: Readings from Scientific America, San Francisco: W.H. Freeman & Co., 1951.

Loew, Clemens, Ph.D. and Silverstone, Barbara, M., MA, A Program of Intensified Stimulation and Response Facilitation for the Senile Aged, Bronx: Daughters of Jacob Geriatric Center, August 1, 1970.

Chapter X

Auserwald, E.H., "Interdisciplinary versus Ecological Approach", Family Process, Vol. 7, 1968.

Halpern, H.A., Canale, J.R., Gant, B.L. and Bellamy, C., "A Systems Crisis Approach to Family Treatment", Journal of Marital and Family Therapy, Vol. 5, No. 2, April 1979.

Howells, J.G., Theory and Practice of Family Therapy, New York: Brunner-Mazel, 1971.

Klein, D.C., Community Dynamics and Mental Health, New York: John Wiley & Sons, 1968.

Meyer, Carol H., "What Directions for Direct Practice", Social Work, Vol. 24, No. 4, July 1979.

National Association of Social Workers - Council on Social Work Education Task Force on Specialization, Specialization in the Social Work Profession, NASW News, No. 24, April 1979.

Schutz, Margaret L. and Gordon, William E., "A Natural Basis for Social Work Specialization", Social Work, Vol. 22, September 1977.

ENDNOTES

Chapter 1

[1]   Bartlett, Harriet, The Common Base of Social Work Practice, New York: National Association of Social Workers, 1970.

[2]   Richmond, Mary, What Is Social Casework?, New York: Russell Sage Foundation, 1922.

[3]   Mullen, Edward J. and Dumpson, James R., eds., Evaluation of Social Intervention. San Francisco: Jossey-Bass, 1976.

[4]   Bartlett, op. cit.

[5]   Meyer, Carol H. "What Directions for Direct Practice?" Social Work, vol. 24, No. 4, July 1979.

[6]   Meyer, Ibid.

[7]   Meyer, Ibid.

Chapter 2

[1]   Uniform Crime Reports, Crime in the United States, 1975. Washington, D.C. U.S. Government Printing Office, 1976.

[2]   Jay R. Williams & Martin Gold, "From Delinquent Behavior to Official Delinquency." Social Problems 20 (Fall 1972), pp. 209-229.

[3]   Philip H. Ennis, "Crimes, Victims, & Police." Transaction 4 (1967), pp. 36-44.

[4]   "Wide Disparities in Crime Totals Found in Sampling of 8 Cities." The New York Times, January 27, 1974, p. 34.

[5]   David Burnham, "New York is Found Safest of 13 Cities in Crime Study." The New York Times, April 15, 1974, p. 1.

[6]   James P. Levine, "The Potential for Crime Overreporting in Criminal Victimization Surveys," Criminology 14 (3) (Nov. 1976), pp. 307-330.

[7]   Reece McGee, ed. Sociology: An Introduction (New York: Holt, Rinehart & Winston, 1980).

[8]   "Are Criminals Made or Born?" The New York Times Magazine, August 4, 1985, p. 31.

[9]   Emile Durkheim, Suicide: A Study in Sociology, trans. John A. Spaulding & George Simpson (New York: Free Press, 1951).

10   Richard J. Herrnstein & James Q. Wilson, op. cit., p. 32.
11   Ibid., p. 32.
12   Donald Light, Jr. & Suzanne Keller, Sociology, 2nd ed. (New York: Alfred M. Knopf, 1979).
13   Alfred K. Cohen, Deviance and Control (Englewood Cliffs, N.J., Prentice-Hall, 1966).
14   Albert Bandura & Richard H. Walters, Adolescent Aggression, New York: Ronald Press, 1959.
15   Reece McGee, op. cit., p. 475.
16   Travis Hirschi, Causes of Delinquency (Berkeley University of California Press, 1971), pp. 3-4.
17   Hirschi, Ibid., pp. 3-4.
18   Emile Durkheim, Suicide, op. cit.
19   Don C. Gibbons & Joseph F. Jones, The Study of Deviance. Englewood Cliffs, N.J.; Prentice-Hall, 1975.
20   Robert K. Merton, Social Theory & Social Structure. Glencoe, Ill.: Free Press, 1947.
21   Merton, ibid., p. 132.
22   Merton, ibid., p. 132.
23   Reece McGee, op. cit., p. 477.
24   Clifford R. Shaw & Henry D. McKay, Delinquency Areas. Chicago, University of Chicago Press, 1929.
25   Edwin H. Sutherland & Donald R. Cressy, Principles of Criminology, 6th ed. Philadelphia - Lippincott, 1960.
26   Donald Light Jr. & Suzanne Keller, op. cit., p. 241.
27   Light and Keller, ibid., p. 241.
28   Walter B. Miller, "Lower-class culture as a generating of gang delinquency," Journal of Sociological Issues, vol. 14, 1958, pp. 15-19.
29   Edward Sutherland, "Differential Association", Wolfgang, Savity & Johnston, eds., The Sociology of Crime and Delinquency, vol. 14, No. 3, 1958.
30   Light and Keller, op. cit., p. 242.
31   Travis Hirschi, op. cit.
32   Travis Hirschi, op. cit.
33   Michael Lewis, "Culture & Gender Roles: There's No Unisex in the Nursery." Psychology Today, vol. 5 (May 1972), pp. 54-57.
34   Herrnstein and Wilson, op. cit., p. 46.
35   Ibid., p. 46.
36   Robbins, Lewis, "Traditional Reductionism Is Unsatisfactory," International Journal of Psychiatry, vol. 7, No. 2, 1969, p. 154.
37   Glassner, Barry & Freedman, Jonathan A. Clinical Sociology. New York and London: Longman, Inc., 1979.

Chapter 3

1   McShane, Claudette, "Community Services for Battered Women," Social Work, vol. 24, No. 1 (January 1979), pp. 34-39.
2   Rosemary Reynolds and Else Siegle, "A Study of Casework with Sadomasochistic Marriage Partners," Social Casework, 40 (December 1959), pp. 545-551.
3   Jane H. Pfouts and Connie Renz, The Future of Wife Abuse Programs," Social Work, 26 (November 1981), pp. 451-455.
4   Willis Kettrell and Allan Mohl, Ph.D., A Needs Assessment of Community District 6 in the South Bronx, TIP Neighborhood House, April '81, (unpublished).
5   Ibid.
6   Cathy Costantino, "Interview with Battered Women: The Lawyer-Social Worker Team," Social Work, 26 (November '81), pp. 456-640.
7   Ibid., p. 458.
8   Ibid., p. 458.
9   Ibid., p. 459.
10 Cook, David R. and Frantz-Cook, Anne. "A Systematic Treatment Approach to Wife Battering," Journal of Marital and Family Therapy, 1984, 10, pp. 83-93.
11 Ibid., p. 89.
12 Margolin, G., "Conjoint Marital Therapy to Enhance Anger Management and Reduce Spouse Abuse." American Journal of Family Therapy, 1981, 7, pp. 675-692.
13 Costantino; op. cit., p. 459.
14 Bonnie E. Carlson, "Battered Women and Their Assailants," Social Work, 22 (November 1977), pp. 455-460.
15 Ibid., p. 460.

Chapter 4

1   Gordon, Thomas Dr., P.E.T. Parent Effectiveness Training: The Tested New Way to Raise Responsible Children, The New American Library, Inc., New York, 1975.
2   Rogers, Carl, "The Necessary and Sufficient Conditions of Therapeutic Personality Change," Journal of Consulting Psychology, Vol. 22 (March 1957), pp. 95-103.
3   Therrien, Mark E. "Evaluating Empathy Skill Training for Parents," Social Work, Vol. 24 (September '79), pp. 417-419.
4   Ibid., p. 419.

5   Carkhuff, Robert R. and Berenson, Bernard G., <u>Beyond Counseling and Therapy</u>, New York, Holt, Rinehart & Winston, 1967.

6   <u>Op. cit.</u>, p. 419.

7   Vattano, Anthony J. "Power to the People: Self-help Groups," <u>Social Work</u>, Vol. 17 (July 1972), pp. 7-15.

8   <u>Ibid.</u>, p. 15.

Chapter 5

1   Kettrell, Willis and Mohl, Allan. <u>Needs Assessment of CD #6 in the South Bronx</u>, Bronx: TIP Neighborhood House, Inc., April 1981.

2   <u>Child Welfare Information Services Print Out Sheet</u>, N.Y.S. Department of Social Services, Albany, New York, 1980.

3   <u>Op. cit.</u>, p. 30.

4   <u>Ibid.</u>, p. 30.

5   <u>Ibid.</u>, p. 31.

Chapter 6

1   DeFrances, Vincent. <u>Protecting the Child Victim of Sex Crimes Committed by Adults</u>. Denver, Colorado: American Humane Association, 1969.

2   Brant, Renee and Tisza, Veronica. "The Sexually Misused Child", <u>American Journal of Orthopsychiatry</u>, Vol. 47, January 1977, pp. 80-90.

3   Shamroy, Jerilyn A., "A Perspective on Childhood Sexual Abuse", <u>Social Work</u>, Vol. 25, March 1980, pp. 128-131.

4   Mohl, Allan M.S.S., <u>A Comparison Study of Three Treatment Models In Dealing with Intra-Familial Child Sexual Abuse</u>. (Mimeo) Jamaica, Queens; Q.S.P.C.C., 1980.

5   Sgroi, Suzanne Ph.D. "The Sexual Assault of Children, Dynamics of the Problem and Abuses in Program Development", <u>Sexual Abuse of Children: Implications From the Sexual Trauma Treatment Program of Connecticut</u>, Community Council of Greater New York, April 1979.

6   <u>Ibid.</u>, p. 26.

7   Zaphiris, Alexander G. Ed.D. <u>Incest: The Family with Two Known Victims</u>. Englewood, Colorado: American Humane Association, 1978.

8   <u>Ibid.</u>, p. 36.

9   Brooks, Barbara. <u>Familial Influences in Father-Daughter Incest</u>. White Plains, New York: New York Hospital - Cornell Medical Center, 1981.

10   "Attacking the Last Taboo". Time, April 14, 1980, p. 72.

11 Giarretto, Henry. "Humanistic Treatment of Father-Daughter Incest", Child Abuse and Neglect: The Family and the Community, Eds: R.E. Helfer & C.H. Kempe, Michigan State University, Ballinger Publications, 1977.

Chapter 7

1 Since paper was written in 1979, it should be noted that the Diagnostic Center houses fewer than 20 children and is no longer in the facility described in paper.
2 Since 1979, 2 additional group homes are now under the umbrella of QSPCC.
3 Warm, Harriet L. "Planning in a Public Child Welfare Agency: A Case Study", Child Welfare. February '78, p. 96.
4 Keith-Lucas, Alan and Sanford, Clifford W. Group Child Care As a Family Service. Chapel Hill: University of North Carolina Press, 1977, p. 43.
5 Schaefer, Charles E. "Some Guidelines on the Effective Use of Punishment," Child Care Quarterly, Vol. 5, No. 4, Winter, 1976, p. 310.
6 Meyer, Margrit, Odom, E.B. and Wax, Bernice S. "Birth and Life of an Incentive System in a Residential Institution for Adolescents." Child Welfare, October '73.
7 QSPCC staff had very high motivation to participate in the point system due to their request for a program of this type.
8 In addition to my duties as Director of Residential Social Services, I functioned for awhile as the Unit Director of Unit A.
9 Ross, Andrew L. "Combining Behavior Modification and Group Work Techniques in a Day Treatment Center," Child Welfare. July 1974, p. 440.

Chapter 8

1 Grossbard, Hyman, Cottage Parents - What They Have to Be, Know, and Do, New York: Child Welfare League of America, Inc., 1972.
2 Ibid.
3 Beker, Jerome, Editorial: "On Defining the Child Care Profession." Child Care Quarterly, 1976, Vol. 5, No. 3, pp. 165-166.
4 Ibid.
5 American Association for Children's Residential Centers, From Chaos to Order: A Collective View of the Residential Treatment of Children, New York: Child Welfare League of America, Inc., 1972.

Chapter 9

[1] Anderson, J.E., "Environment and Meaningful Activity," in Williams, Tibbett, and Donahue (Eds.) Processes of The Aging, Vol. 1, New York: Atherton Press, 1963, pp. 223-244.

[2] Catti, S.H., "Some Dynamics of Middle and Later Years," Smith College Studies in Social Work (Vol. 33), February 1963, pp. 121-124.

[3] Heron, W., "The Pathology of Boredom," in Coopersmith, S. (Ed.), Frontiers of Psychological Research, Readings from Scientific America, San Francisco: W.H. Freeman & Co., 1951.

[4] Loew, Clemens, Ph.D. and Silverstone, Barbara, M., MA, A Program of Intensified Stimulation and Response Facilitation for the Senile Aged (unpublished), Daughters of Jacob Geriatric Center, Bronx, August 1, 1970.

[5] Ibid., p. 10.

[6] Berkman, Barbara. Mental Health and the Aging: A Review of the Literature for Clinical Social Workers. Clinical Social Work Journal, 1978, Vol. 6, No. 3, pp. 230-249.

[7] Loew and Silverstone, op. cit., pp. 23-24.

[8] Butler, R.N. "Psychiatry and the Elderly: An Overview." The American Journal of Psychiatry, 1975, Vol. 132, No. 9, pp. 893-900.

Chapter 10

[1] Ford, Donald H. and Urban, Hugh B., eds., Systems of Psychotherapy: A Comparative Study. New York: John Wiley & Sons, Inc., 1964.

[2] Speck, R. "Psychotherapy of the Social Network of a Schizophrenic Family." Family Process, Vol. 6, 1967.

[3] Auserwald, E.H. "Interdisciplinary versus Ecological Approach." Family Process, Vol. 7, 1968, pp. 109-114.

[4] Saranson, S.B. "Community Psychology, Networks and Mr. Everyman." American Psychologist, Vol. 11, 1976, pp. 317-328.

[5] Klein, D.C. Community Dynamics and Mental Health. New York: John Wiley & Sons, 1968.

[6] Howell, J.G. Theory and Practice of Family Therapy, New York: Brunner/ Magel, 1971.

[7] Op. cit., p. 5.

[8] Halpern, H.A., Canale, J.K., Gant, B.L. and Bellamy, C. "A Systems-Crisis Approach to Family Treatment." Journal of Marital and Family Therapy, Vol. 5, No. 2, April 1979.

[9] Ibid., p. 88.

[10]   We are describing the Queensboro Society for the Prevention of Cruelty to Children's Diagnostic Center which was located in Jamaica, New York.

[11]   Meyer, Carol H., "What Direction for Direct Practice," Social Work, Vol. 24, No. 4, July 1979, pp. 270-271.

[12]   Ibid., p. 272.

[13]   National Association of Social Workers - Council on Social Work Education Task Force on Specialization, "Specialization in the Social Work Profession," NASW News, 24 (April '79), pp. 20 and 31.

[14]   William Gordon and Margaret L. Schutz, "A Natural Basis for Social Work Specialization," Social Work, Vol. 22, Sept. '77, pp. 422-426.

[15]   Ibid., pp. 422-426.

[16]   Carol Meyer, op. cit.

[17]   Meyer, ibid., p. 272.

Printed in the United States
By Bookmasters